Talking with Tech Leads

From Novices to Practitioners

Patrick Kua
Foreword by Jim Webber

Talking with Tech Leads
From Novices to Practitioners

Patrick Kua

This book is for sale at
http://leanpub.com/talking-with-tech-leads

This version was published on 2014-12-30

ISBN 150581748X

©2013 - 2014 Patrick Kua

Also By Patrick Kua
The Retrospective Handbook

Contents

Foreword i

Preface v
   Why I wrote this book v
   What you'll find in this book vi

Acknowledgements ix

Testimonials xi

Introduction 1
   In the Beginning 1
   From Tech Leads to Tech Leads 4
   From Novices to Practitioners 6

Novices 11
   A Different Perspective – Cameron Swords . 21
   Change of Focus – Anne Simmons 25
   Needs for a Wider Skill Set – Ebony Pierce . 29
   Juggling Act – Siebert Lubbe 34

CONTENTS

    The External Face – Liz Douglass 39
    Chaos and Cluelessness – Roy Osherove . . . 42
    More Than Just Tech – Priyank Gupta 45
    The Bigger Picture – Suchit Puri 57
    Less Coding, More Responsibility – David 'Bucky' Schwarz 61
    Lean on Communication Skills – Stefan Marev 65

Practitioners 73

People 75
    Team Focus – Alison Rosewarne 80
    Team over Self – Humphrey Elton 84
    Delegate, Delegate, Delegate – Jason Selby . 90
    Facilitating, then Leading – Dan Abel 95
    Helping the Team – Adam Esterline 101
    Inwards and Outwards – Rachel Laycock . . 104
    Soft Skills – Jon Pither 111
    Enabling People – Isabella Degen 116
    It's Not About the Code – Patric Fornasier . 122
    People Focus – Sarah Taraporewalla 127
    Engaging the Team – Glen Ford 131

The Tech of a Tech Lead 137
    Teams and Architecture – Simon Brown . . . 142
    Enablement and Solution Design – Marten Gustafson 147
    Manage Tech Debt – Mark Crossfield 153

An Architect Too? – Tomi Vanek 159
  Champion Quality – Peter Moran 164
  Don't Forget Cross-Functional Requirements
     – Christy Allmon 168
  Prioritising Tech Tasks – Chris Close 174

Bridging the Business with Tech 179
  The Big Picture – Luca Grulla 186
  Align Technology with Business – Robert
     Annett 192
  Mapping the Future – Jason Dennis 195
  Finding Balance with the Business – Cory Foy 198
  A Bridge to the Business – Ryan Kinderman 202

You 211
  Managing Yourself – Stephen Hardisty . . . 216
  Scouting – Geoffrey Giesemann 224
  Lead from Behind – Joel Tosi 230
  Understand Yourself – Daniel Worthington-
     Bodart 236
  Finding Balance – Laura Paterson 239

Conclusions 245
  Lessons Learned by First-Time Tech Leads . . 246
  Lessons Learned by Practising Tech Leads . . 248
  Final Words 253

Appendix 255
  Useful Books 255

CONTENTS

Useful Websites 258
Other References 259

About the Author **261**

Foreword

By Jim Webber, Chief Scientist, Neo4j
http://jimwebber.org[1]
@jimwebber[2]

When Patrick approached me to write this foreword, I was a little hesitant. I'm not especially renowned – not even as a Tech Lead! But after I read the book, I began to understand why Patrick believed I'd find the book worthy of a small contribution.

This is an important book and it makes a substantial contribution to the soft side of software: namely one that begins a path towards empirical reflection on what it means to be a senior software engineer. Moreover, in "Talking with Tech Leads" Patrick has captured a wide variety of experiences, opinions, and reflections on what it means to bear the responsibilities of a Tech Lead, far beyond "merely" being competent at software delivery.

[1] http://jimwebber.org
[2] http://www.twitter.com/jimwebber

Uncovering the practices, emotions, and ambitions of Tech Leads as well as their doubts, uncertainties and tribulations is a valuable first step towards empirically qualifying the nature and expectations of the role. In taking that step, it enables the new Tech Lead to manage their own expectations (and nerves) and the seasoned Tech Lead to grow through understanding how their peers have solved (or failed to solve) the challenges that beset others.

This is not a career guidance book, or even a self-help book, though both I think are suitably addressed as a side-effect of reading and internalising the interviews. This is a book that you can turn to when you're feeling unsure about moving into, or expanding your role as a Tech Lead. It provides an immediate sense of community, global and diverse, by the nature of the interviewees. Their stories resonate precisely because they're honest accounts from representative technologists, much like you, the reader. All are well catalogued and curated to be engaging and provide an overarching narrative that maps conveniently to a typical career arc.

I expect, like most software people, ordinarily I read technical works much more than I read experience reports. "Talking with Tech Leads" has helped me redress some of that balance and think through what it means to lead software teams in the early 21st century. For that I am grateful to Patrick and I hope you'll feel that the book will help you to reflect upon, and address, your challenges and aspirations around technical leadership too.

Preface

Why I wrote this book

I have played the Tech Lead role countless times, in my role as a software development consultant at ThoughtWorks. In over a decade of working in IT, I have seen how different Tech Leads operate and grapple with their difficult problems. I have also trained, coached and successfully developed other Tech Leads – both within ThoughtWorks and for the clients we work with. I noticed that the transition for a developer to a Tech Lead is never easy. Even experienced Tech Leads struggle when they first change teams or organisations.

When you, the developer, become a Tech Lead, you suddenly realise how lonely the role is. You will no longer be "just a developer," and you will no longer be treated as such. When you look for support and advice, you find that no one can understand your unique position, team and context. If you work for a larger organisation, you are in luck – you have other Tech Leads around you. But even then, you cannot easily see how they run their teams and even less likely, how they think through the problems they face.

I started this book project because I saw how developers struggled to adapt to the different skills and responsibilities that come with the Tech Lead title. The experience you gain as a developer does not prepare you for the responsibilities of the role. Unlike the bountiful number of books on programming, there are few resources that help developers prepare for this role, or help Tech Leads develop themselves further.

This book helps you on your journey to becoming a better Tech Lead.

What you'll find in this book

This book offers you the experiences from real-life Tech Leads. I wanted this book to represent a wide spectrum of experiences and found Tech Leads who work all over the world in different circumstances.

Some Tech Lead works for very large organisations, whilst others work for very small groups. Their teams write software in industries such as travel, finance, real estate, media, and consulting. Some Tech Leads guide a team of very experienced developers, whilst others lead a team with a mix of experience, including developers relatively new to the industry. With this spectrum, I hope there are people you can relate to, and also new circumstances to be aware of in the role of a Tech Lead.

The Tech Leads share their views their role and how they solve problems through a series of curated interviews. The structure of the interviews was intentionally similar, in order to see how different Tech Leads responded.

You will find that there is no single *best* way to lead development teams. Instead, you will discover different approaches to dealing with different aspects of the Tech Lead role.

Acknowledgements

First of all, I would like to thank all the contributors. I know how time-consuming the Tech Lead role is and it took significant number of hours for each person to think about and write down their thoughts about the role. Sharing stories about tough times requires humility and everyone offered their experiences to share and learn from.

I'd like to give special thanks to contributors in the *Novice* section of the book. Not only were they hard to source, because being a Tech Lead for the first time happens only once of course, but they were also courageous in sharing their experiences with the world.

Thanks too to the countless people who helped put me in touch with the people included in the book. Without their recommendations and people they introduced me to, I would not have been able to pass on such a wide variety of experiences and backgrounds.

I recognise that the contents may be a little biased with many people having some connection with Thought-

Works[3]. This is down to my background and network. I worked conscientiously to cast my net further afield, attempting to capture Tech Leads working in a diverse set of companies, industries, and with a broad range of experiences. I hope that as a reader you benefit from this.

I'd also like to thank the editor I collaborated with, Angela Jameson Potts of Virtual Editor[4]. It was a great pleasure to work with her again, and I greatly appreciated her flexible approach to working with very non-traditional book formatting tools.

Finally, I want to acknowledge you, the reader: thank you for selecting this book. I hope you learn much from it.

---

[3]http://www.thoughtworks.com
[4]http://www.virtualeditor.co.uk/

Testimonials

"I wish I had read this book five years ago. It changed the way I worked the day after I read it. I would recommend it to any new or aspiring Tech Lead."

– David Morgantini, Tech Lead, UK Government Digital Service

"Reading 'Talking with Tech Leads' is like going to a conference and watching a great panel discussion on leading teams."

"This book has made me rethink my position and the way I work with my direct reports."

– Nick Malnick, Tech Lead, DRW Trading Group

"I like the evolution of advice, comments and interviews and increasing depth and complexity generated by the book structure."

– Hugo Corbucci, Tech Lead, ThoughtWorks

Introduction

In the Beginning

Technical Leaders – Tech Leads for short – almost all start out in the same way: a programmer or software developer, either by circumstance or through the passing of time, who is asked to take on the Tech Lead role. The story often goes something like this:

Meet Brian. Brian works as a developer for Zalana, a company selling a software-as-a-service product to people who work in Human Resources. Brian has been with Zalana since its start, three years ago.

Over the years, the development team has grown from just Brian to three other developers. The other developers really respect Brian for his ability to design,

test and write robust code that is also easy to understand. Sheryl, the Product Manager, drives the product direction and almost always approaches Brian when she has questions because she finds he communicates well with her. He is particularly good at explaining technical solutions or constraints to her.

One day, the founder of Zalana, Bob invited Brian out for breakfast. Brian thought this a little unusual because he knew Bob never ate breakfast and preferred to spend time late into the evenings with investors and potential customers. Intrigued and slightly concerned, Brian agreed to meet Bob at a cosy French restaurant. Brian arrives, sees Bob on his smartphone, reading and responding to emails, and sits down opposite.

Bob sees Brian approach and puts down his smartphone. Bob smiles, waiting for Brian to sit before announcing, "Brian, I have some exciting news. Our business is doing well. We have just signed three big customers. I know the development team has been working hard. We can really see the results, but we need to grow the team; double or triple it if need be." Bob pauses to scan Brian's face. "We want you to take the Tech Lead role."

Brian's mind is reeling at the prospect of three new customers and the fresh stream of demands on the development team, as well as the offer of a new role.

Questions race through his head: Why me? What will investors and the rest of the business expect of me? How will the other developers see me? Will I still get to write code?

Brian knows Bob's impatient but good nature and answers, "OK, I'll give it a go." But, as Bob orders another coffee, Brian looks at his menu and thinks, "Now what?"

Although this is pure fiction, it illustrates the lesson underlying many of the interviews in this book. The Tech Lead role is quite distinct from the developer role, even though they overlap to some degree. However, those who move into the role are always surprised at what the differences are. Like Brian, many find themselves thrust into the role of a Tech Lead by chance or opportunity, and it was only when they found themselves in the Tech Role that they realised the different responsibilities required many skills that you don't develop in the role of a programmer.

The time you spend honing your development skills, such as seeing patterns in code, refactoring code to be easier to maintain or extend, and writing tests does little to prepare skills in resolving conflict, establishing a team culture, or communicating technology in ways that non-technical people can understand.

Tech Leads almost always find themselves working

solo and the question *"Am I doing the right things as a Tech Lead?"* is often difficult to answer. Most developers have other developers to ask for their opinion on which tool or framework to use, or to get feedback on the design or testability of their code. A Tech Lead rarely has other Tech Leads around to share ideas on approaching people problems, or ways to more effectively communicate pressing technical matters to the business.

This collection of interviews provides that missing link: how others approach the role, the challenges they have and the different experiences demonstrate the ways people succeed in different ways as a Tech Lead.

From Tech Leads to Tech Leads

For the purposes of this book, I define a Tech Lead as:

> A leader, responsible for a development team, who spends at least 30 per cent of their time writing code with the team.

I feel that writing *some* code is an important aspect of technical leadership. Having a technical background is not usually enough to help facilitate discussions or mitigate technical risk. Some organisations have roles like *Technical Manager*, *Development Manager* or *Team Lead* and people in these roles do not write any code. This book does not attempt to describe their responsibilities or challenges.

This book focuses solely on giving advice to software developers who suddenly find themselves dealing with significantly, but not exclusively non-technical tasks. Suddenly, when given the Tech Lead role, a developer is required to balance new non-technical tasks with their familiar world of detailed design, solving software problems (not people problems!) and cutting code.

Although many people could have given responses to what they feel a Tech Lead does or should do, I wanted to collect lessons and experiences from real Tech Leads. The contributors I have included in this book match two simple criteria:

1. They are responsible for a team of more than three developers;
2. They write code with the team.

These two factors excluded many who would typically bear titles such as Software Architect, Team

Manager, Development Manager, Head of Development, or Agile Coach. The people playing these roles may have very good ideas and opinions but I wanted to avoid the old adage:

> Do as I say, not as I do.

Rather than giving you ideas that may not have been tried and tested, I offer you stories and lessons learned from people with *real world experience*, people who were playing the Tech Lead role at the time of their interview.

From Novices to Practitioners

The people in this book represent two perspectives that provide the best insight into the Tech Lead role.

- **Novices** - You will not be the first developer to transition into the Tech Lead role. The people interviewed in the Novices section share how they deal with the transition from writing code all day, to suddenly being responsible and accountable for a whole new set of unfamiliar tasks. Each person in this section described

themselves as a "first-time Tech Lead" at the time of the interviews.
- **Practitioners** - First-time Tech Leads quickly transition into experienced Tech Leads in the course of time. While the Tech Lead continues to encounter unique situations they did not experience as a developer, they can draw on other situations they have dealt with previously as a Tech Lead. The people in this section have often played Tech Lead for several teams, or have played the Tech Lead for several years. They share their wisdom and insights they gleaned while gaining more experience in this role.

Finding seasoned Tech Leads proved significantly easier than first-time Tech Leads, and the uneven weighting between the two sections reflects that. With significantly more responses from seasoned Tech Leads, I found several stronger themes emerged and I grouped the responses into:

1. People – Focuses on the softer skills required by the role of Tech Lead.
2. The Tech of a Tech Lead – Outlines different technical responsibilities, which distinguish the Tech Lead from simply being a technical manager.

3. Bridging Business with Tech – Highlights a different perspective and more outward-looking focus.
4. You – Contains responses that relate to you, as an individual, in the role of a Tech Lead.

I have attempted to break down the responses into these different themes, adding in some of my own experiences and observations about what emerged in the responses. I hope the themes enable you to get understand and navigate the various dimensions of the Tech Lead role and hopefully they will make it easier for you to refer back to in the future.

The next page shows a word cloud based on the responses in this book. The word cloud contains keywords that recur frequently and highlights further themes that emerged from the interviews. You may notice that some of the words in large type correspond with the overall themes that emerged, including frequent use of the word "people" as well as thinking about "code".

9

Novices

"In the beginner's mind there are many possibilities; in the expert's mind there are few." – Shunryu Suzuki *Zen Mind, Beginner's Mind*

The stories in this section demonstrate the most significant differences that developers discover when they move into the role of Tech Lead. Their views are important because they highlight the challenges that developers face and how they must adapt and find the skills required for their new role.

With a better understanding of the key contrast areas, organisations and management can provide more support to people transitioning to these roles through targeted training and coaching.

A Wider Outlook

Developers deal with the small details all the time. They must be sure not to forget that semi-colon, that extra comma, or some other special symbol that will make the difference between something working and failing. Implementing features correctly means focusing on detail in the present. Good developers think about designing their feature and how it fits into the broader context; Tech Leads spend much of their time thinking about the broader context.

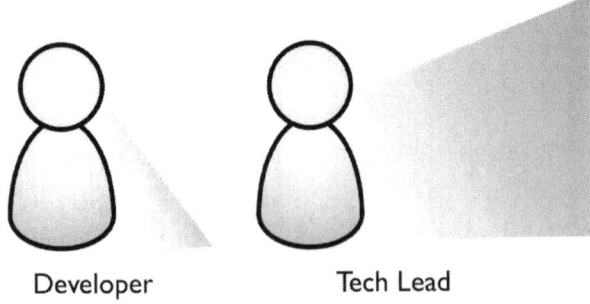

Developer · Tech Lead

Differences in perspective

A Tech Lead spends much more time thinking about the future state of the system, and the impact that adding a feature today will have on adding features tomorrow. A 'good enough' design and implementation is not one where the original developer is the only person able to understand and maintain it. It is the job of the Tech Lead to consider whether or not the entire development group will be able to understand and shape it.

As people in this chapter observe, the Tech Lead has to spend more time seeing the bigger picture; thinking about the future consequences of today's decisions. The choice of a new programming language to tackle a problem might be the easiest and most appropriate to one developer on the team, for example, but the Tech Lead is aware of the potential challenges it could throw up in the deployment environment, such as having the new programming language available on all machines; making sure the entire team can understand and maintain the same codebase; the time that may have to be spent on developing new skills.

Choices are no longer evaluated in terms of 'this works for me', but the broader ecosystem. The Tech Lead evaluates a decision in terms of the consequences it will have for other parties. They spend more time considering questions such as:

- Does this choice limit what we can do for the business or product manager?
- Can other members of the team understand and change or extend the design?
- Will making this choice threaten the performance or user-experience for end-users?
- Does this choice simply shift work to other parties in our organisation and is that beneficial for the business?

- Will this design create more work in the long run?

Sensing Greater Responsibility

> *"With great power comes great responsibility"* - Uncle Ben from *Spiderman*

Organisations often designate Tech Leads as a point of authority. Other parts of the organisation trust the Tech Lead to lead their team to success and this brings with it accountability to the rest of the organisation.

A Product Manager may ask the Tech Lead to work with the rest of the team to find the solution to a problem, for example, but ultimately, it is the Tech Lead who will be called upon to explain why it is the best solution or what the consequences of a choice might be.

When they move into the role of Tech Lead, developers find themselves closer to the rest of the business. They become more aware of the time-sensitive aspect of making decisions, because the timing may directly affect the ability of the business to make money and these have to align.

Guiding the Technical Vision

The Tech Lead attempts to bring team members closer together, so they see things in the same light. The Tech Lead appreciates how everyone approaches problems differently. They invest time in helping the team understand the Technical Vision so the entire team is pulling together in the same direction. The Tech Lead realises they are ultimately responsible for steering the group.

Over time, the Tech Lead starts to recognise how differently people can interpret the same message and has to find alternative ways of communicating the same idea to avoid misunderstandings. Some people may understand an idea after talking about it; some need time to absorb the idea and respond, and yet others find a diagram on a white board easier to read because they depend on visualisation.

As one interviewee succinctly said:

> "Communication takes time."

Less Time for Writing Code

As I defined in the introduction to this book, I would expect Tech Leads to spend at least 30 per cent of their time coding. I wouldn't expect them to be writing code all the time because they have considerably more responsibilities. The Tech Lead spends less time writing code because of the effort required to zoom out from the fine detail to the bigger picture and to think about the impact that today's decision has on the future.

Time not spent coding may be spent helping other developers on problem-solving, perhaps connecting them with other developers in the team because a different skill set or approach is needed, or helping connect them with people outside of the team. Tech Leads often (but not always!) have more experience than some of the developers and so naturally, some of their time will be spent teaching. The Tech Lead also spends time looking not just at code smells[5], but also observing team interactions and environmental constraints that hinder the team.

Tech Leads have less time to spend on writing code because they are expected to interact with other roles in the organisation. Building relationships with other people in the organisation takes time and it usually means the Tech Lead needs to attend many more meetings than the rest of the team.

Many novices I interviewed struggled with the tran-

---

[5]http://en.wikipedia.org/wiki/Code_smell

sition into the Tech Lead role because they had less time to write code. As a developer, you perceive the value you add in terms of the functionality you enable through the code that you write. When you take on the Tech Lead role, this value is threatened because other tasks draw you away from writing code.

I too struggled with this until I realised that the way the Tech Lead brings value is completely different. The Tech Lead brings value by enabling everyone on the team to contribute code as much as possible; by avoiding rewrites due to people working in different ways; by managing technical debt to make it easier to add code, and by promoting relationships between the development group and business colleagues to ensure the code addresses business goals and delivers true value. As a leader, you enable others to do their work; you harmonise and thereby maximise the efforts of the entire group, not just an individual.

Juggling More Context Switches

The people in this section talk about picking up new responsibilities in addition to building a technical solution. They found themselves in more meetings, needing to rise to abstract levels, or helping people solve different problems in a completely different part of the system.

The role of a Tech Lead often requires more context switching, which can certainly be frustrating when you first step into the role. Learning better time-management and task-management techniques as well as delegation skills will help you to cope.

Allowing People to Fail

> *"Learning is the bottleneck in software development"* Anonymous

By the time you move into the Tech Lead role you will have spent some time in the industry working as a developer. You will have made some mistakes, learned from them and, hopefully, be able to guard yourself against practices to avoid. When other people are about to make mistakes, you will want to jump in because you want to help avoid them. You may convince them to use a different solution, but unfortunately, the next time a similar problem arises, they may not remember to take that course of action.

A hard lesson for the Tech Lead is allowing people to fail, allowing them to make mistakes. Failure is a natural part of the learning process; it forces you to evaluate circumstances and try again. Directing people to a solution avoids failure altogether. Some people are able to learn if you articulate the alternatives and the thought process behind the solution, but in my experience, not many people can learn this way.

Create safety by reducing the time for feedback. Perhaps at the start of a new task, you check in with a person daily to see how they are approaching the problem and to ask questions to get them to see trade-offs in their solution. Allow them to try their own approaches, but if you sense it is heading in the wrong direction, find ways to let them see that for themselves.

Asking the right questions, deciding when to check-in – not too often and not for too long – are skills that take time to develop.

People Aspects are Hard

People I interviewed in this section wrote about the surprisingly difficult side to people management. As a developer, you see the people you work with as colleagues, as individuals. When you become a Tech Lead, harmonising the team requires you to spend time understanding individuals and focus on improving interactions between the individuals.

Working with a computer is a complete contrast to working with people. Computers do not talk back and are not (usually) temperamental. You can work with a computer instantly, whereas it takes time to build trust with people. Computers continue to do their work until they break, while people have lives outside of work that may affect their moods and how well they do their job.

You are a person too, and as a Tech Lead you must be aware of your own mood and emotions. The team will watch, observe, and judge every word you utter and every action you make, whether or not you like it or want it. You need to consider your choice of words and actions carefully as people can quickly misread and misinterpret what you intend.

A Different Perspective – Cameron Swords

Describe what responsibilities the Tech Lead has

From a technical perspective, my role included:

- Setting out a technical vision that aligned with the business vision (although this was pretty much done)
- Helping communicate technical issues, problems, and solutions to stakeholders
- Managing releases - determining what we're releasing, when, and what's possible

From a leadership perspective, my role included:

- Ensuring everyone moved in the same direction; towards the same vision
- Understanding each developer's goals, interests, and strengths

- Supporting people by challenging them in a way appropriate to their skills

Does the role of Tech Lead hold any surprises?

The Tech Lead role gave me the opportunity to view the team from the perspective of an "outsider". Working on and with teams as an "insider", I would often be quite critical of people and the decisions made; it affected how I felt about our success as a team.

Having an outside perspective meant I could understand how other people measure the team's success. It was very different from my own.

The pros and cons

I definitely had more influence on both the technical vision and the way the team was run. Holding the "authority stick" means there is less chance of someone else using the "authority stick" on you. That gave me more opportunity to empower people in the trenches.

I spent less time coding. I'd like to think I would code more if I worked with a more senior team. I also found that managing people is not what makes me happy. Building solutions that enable people is what makes me happy. So there are parts of the Tech Lead role that you just "have" to do.

Any preparation advice?

I feel like I spent a lot of time "preparing". At some point, I think you just need to jump in and play the role of Tech Lead.

I do notice some developers (some very junior) say they would like to be a Tech Lead. I would like to find a way to give them a better understanding of what the role is, so they can make a more informed judgment about their career.

Where do you go for support?

The former Tech Lead (*this book's editor*) was on my project and mentored me. My team was very supportive of me, particularly when I first started. I also found the *Tech Lead lunches* useful.

> *What is a Tech Lead lunch?*
>
> We held lunches inviting either existing Tech Leads or people interesting in being a Tech Lead. In this informal setting, we discussed challenging situations, asked each other questions about concerns as a Tech Lead and offered each other different ways to approach problems.

Has your perspective changed?

As a developer, I keep my head up a lot more now to try and support the leaders in the team.

Cameron's key question: I've no idea what the question is! Here is what I want to answer.

Taking one of the most experienced programmers out of the team to be the Tech Lead is a broken model. I am passionate about fixing it. Given more time and opportunity in the role, this is what I'll be trying to do.

Cameron's background story

Cameron studied Computer Science at the University of Sydney and joined ThoughtWorks as a graduate seven years ago. He most recently spent two months playing the Tech Lead role with a team of about 12 developers.

Change of Focus – Anne Simmons

Does the role of Tech Lead hold any surprises?

The biggest difference for me so far is the change in focus, as you need to focus more on the overall vision. You still have to focus on small tasks such as developing features and maintaining quality. At the same time, you have to quickly switch from that micro view to a more macro view of the project.

You need to consider a feature's impact on the overall system architecture, spend more time guiding the direction of features and giving input into upcoming work. I have found that you need to switch contexts fairly frequently, and often swiftly, as people come to you for help or questions.

The pros and cons

I enjoy the sense of responsibility. I enjoy being in a position to help people untangle problems, and figuring out how to get the best out of everyone. I also enjoy being part of the planning process for future work and the increased engagement with other roles.

What I found hard was knowing what to worry about, and what not to. I still find it difficult to work out which 'smells' to focus on in the short term, and which ones are okay to defer worrying about. I think a lot of this comes with experience. I have come to realise that you can't tackle or worry about everything at once and it is a challenge for me to let go enough for things to sort themselves out, which they often do. I find it is easy to get overwhelmed with all the different aspects of the role.

Any preparation advice?

On my previous team, we introduced the role of Feature Lead. A Feature Lead takes responsibility for the direction and completion of a whole feature. They take part in the analysis, domain modelling and architecture, as well as part of the development. I think this is a great way to get exposure to some of the Tech Lead responsibilities without actually *being* the Tech Lead.

Where do you go for support?

I try to get the most out of the great Tech Leads on my team. I ask to attend some of the activities they run, and ask them to explain the thought processes behind why and how they prioritise and make decisions.

It would be great if there were some kind of magical training course or book that told you how to be a great

Tech Lead; at the moment, you seem to just get thrown into the role and have to figure it out along the way.

Has your perspective changed?

After playing the role of Tech Lead role once, I try to make sure that, as a developer, I understand how the element I am working on fits into the bigger picture of the application. I think more about how it contributes to the wider strategy and purpose.

I also try more to get involved with adjacent teams and planning of stories so that it is not all up to the Tech Lead.

Anne's key question: What do you feel that the role of a Tech Lead entails?

I think everyone has different expectations of a Tech Lead. Some people want a command-and-control style. They want a technical person who will tell them how to do everything. Others want someone who will lead the team and help them become a better working unit. All types of people can make great Tech Leads, as long as they are surrounded by people with complementary strengths. But, if you are one type of lead and people are expecting, or wanting, another type of Tech Lead, fulfilling the role can be hard.

Anne's background story

Anne graduated from Queen's University (Belfast) and joined ThoughtWorks as a graduate, working in Canada, all over the US and in the UK. She is currently a senior developer, working as part of a mixed-discipline development team. She has, more recently, started to take more of a lead role in the development team, leading the design in feature areas or filling in for the Tech Lead when they are away.

She feels like the role is a natural progression as she enjoys mentoring, coaching others and building bonds within and between teams.

Before joining IT, she moonlighted as a ski instructor!

Needs for a Wider Skill Set – Ebony Pierce

Does the role of Tech Lead hold any surprises?

The primary difference between my role as developer and my role as Tech Lead is the focus of projects. As a developer, I was responsible for my role and my designated project deadlines. My concern was always team oriented, making sure that everyone working on the project was able to meet the project deadline, but my focus was primarily on projects that I was working on.

As a Tech Lead, I have to be not only goal-oriented, but also people-oriented. Where I used to be responsible for only my work, I suddenly became responsible for the work of several developers and multiple projects: ensuring that deadlines are not slipping; motivating developers to press forward but checking they are not stretched too thinly; ensuring that moral is not slipping; watching my tone and considering the way information is communicated; ensuring developers have the resources to get their projects completed, and that resources are managed appropriately.

A few of the challenges that I have include: going from managing my own work to the work of others; going from working alongside developers for years to managing them; monitoring how I speak to individuals to minimise misunderstandings; drawing a distinct line between professional and personal, and having to reframe conversations and situations so as not to offend anyone. The hardest part, in my mind, is the shift from working alongside people to managing them. It is sometimes difficult to separate the two, because as a team player, you cover for a co-worker if you know they are lacking, but as a lead, you are responsible for getting things done and you really have to change the way you look at things.

The pros and cons

One of the things that I like about the Tech Lead role is that I have the opportunity to see the whole picture. I see how the day-to-day work interacts with the contract and company, and how my contributions and the contributions of the developers directly affect the success of the entire company.

Honestly, the thing I dislike most about the role is dealing with people. For a long time, I have worked with computers: you tell them exactly what you want and they complete a task. It is difficult to transition into a role where you manage people, because people do not work like computers. If you tell a person something they are not receptive to, several things could result: they may do what is requested; they may say they'll do what is requested, then underperform or take a passive-aggressive approach; they may simply not do what is requested. It is difficult to adapt your approach for each individual based on personality and temperament, whereas for a computer, the language is always the same; they do not read into tone or body language: as long as your directions are specific, the task is completed.

Any preparation advice?

I think that the best thing to prepare for this role would have been a degree in psychology, with a focus on body language reading and non-verbal communication, and a solid poker face. As I don't have that, I think a varied experience is important. The best characteristics of a Tech Lead include adaptability, agility, competence, character, reliability, trustworthiness, and definitely a thick skin. None of these are technical skills that can be taught; they can only be developed with practice and from exposure to different experiences and situations. Tech Leads have to push themselves into challenges and difficult situations, take stretch assignments outside their comfort zone, and practise leading meetings and presentations. Tech Leads have to learn to keep emotions out of the equation and maintain objectivity.

Where do you go for support?

I draw support from different mentors, most of whom are men. I use them as soundboards for ideas, to provide a male perspective of my methods and approach and to help me to understand how male co-workers might perceive my actions. I also draw support from my family and friends: focus and objective. I have several female mentors to turn to for advice and inspiration. I am learning to find an appropriate work-life balance, and to maintain this I take regular vacations where I focus on me. These provide opportunity for me to renew and "store up" self-support for a later date.

Has your perspective changed?

As a developer, I've always tried to have a complete understanding of the system that I was working on and I've tried to be prompt as far as deadlines are concerned. I would not have done anything differently. For other developers considering the transition to Tech Lead at some point, my suggestion would be to ask why. It takes about five whys to get to the root cause of an issue; to identify what needs to be improved and to gain a better understanding of what needs to be done.

Developers who are looking to branch out need to:

- Be curious
- Be thorough
- Read everything
- Maintain objectivity
- Understand the big picture.

Ebony's key question: How do you maintain the drive to continue with such an arduous job?

I maintain the drive from the secure knowledge that my contribution matters and that other people are directly affected by my contribution. It sounds lame, but it's true.

Ebony's background story

Ebony started in IT as a Software Developer building a website using classic ASP, JavaScript, CSS and HTML. At the time of this interview, she was working on a team of nine people and graduated into the role of a Tech Lead after working with her team for several years. Although she didn't have a background in .Net technologies, she won her team over with three months of focused self-study and research.

Juggling Act – Siebert Lubbe

My view of the Tech Lead role

I think it's my responsibility as Tech Lead to lead the team in good software design and architecture. We make most design decisions together as a team, but it is my responsibility to facilitate the design sessions and ensure that what we produce is of high quality and aligned with the organisation's technical vision.

Mentoring the team and team members in good software engineering is also part of what I take on. I spend time with individuals and the team as a whole to discuss code quality, best practices and design decisions. Our software infrastructure is increasingly complex, so I try to be available to new team members to introduce the different aspects of our systems.

We operate in a continuous delivery model. I take ownership of our build and deployment pipelines and ensure that these parts of our development process support our delivery requirements. We are also keen adopters of agile practices, so I ensure that we stay true to this way of working during the development process.

Communicating takes up a big part of my day. I liaise constantly with the business analyst and iteration manager to ensure that our team is aligned with the product vision and broader business direction. I also spend significant time communicating our technical direction with external stakeholders. Our development team is one of many in our organisation that work constantly on the same infrastructure and code bases; it is part of my responsibility to maintain communication with these development teams and their Tech Leads to co-ordinate development efforts, release activities and design decisions.

I am still a programmer at heart. I love writing code and I make it a priority. I believe that staying hands-on is the best way to understand our full stack and enable me to lead our team technically.

Does the role of Tech Lead hold any surprises?

As a developer, I was usually able to focus on one task at a time; as Tech Lead I often have a few things going on at the same time. The number of interruptions I have to deal with on any particular day has increased significantly. This calls for frequent context switches. I sometimes find it difficult to measure my own efficiency and progress. Learning how best to manage my personal time is an ongoing journey.

The pros and cons

I really enjoy seeing the bigger picture across all aspects, including product, business and technology, and being involved in shaping the bigger picture. It is very rewarding to be in a position where I can influence technology decisions to best achieve business requirements.

I also get great satisfaction from leading a team towards a common technical vision. Facilitating technical discussions and motivating the team to technical excellence is something I enjoy a lot.

Being very much a developer at heart, I have found it hard to get used to the reality of writing less code. On the flipside, however, the experience has opened my eyes to a number of new areas and challenges in software development that I find very exciting.

Any preparation advice?

I feel that I have had experience in most of the areas where I require skills: leading a team, understanding our organisation's systems infrastructure, time management, software architecture skills, and agile methodologies. However, more experience would always have been better, and I might have focused a bit more on these areas had I known what was going to be required of me later.

I think it is important to have a mentor from the beginning. I have support now, but I didn't to start with. I would recommend anyone moving into the Tech Lead role to seek mentorship from an individual that they respect and trust.

Where do you go for support?

My line manager has been helpful in defining the expectations for my role and setting objectives to address my skill gaps as I was settling into the new role. This has been a great source of support. I have found that discussions with my line manager are most constructive when I am honest and clear about which areas I would like to improve my skill set in.

Discussing my role and current challenges with colleagues outside of my immediate team is also helpful. This could mean a simple ad hoc chat over a coffee or booking a fortnightly meeting. In my case, there have been two individuals that I respect a lot: one a peer with a little more experience than I; the other a senior with quite a few years of experience and a wealth of knowledge.

Has your perspective changed?

I am more aware of the bigger picture now and of how what we do contributes to the organisation. My perspective has changed about what is a valuable investment of time and effort towards technical and ultimately business vision. I have always valued clever engineering solutions, but I am increasingly aware that good software design decisions lead to more future-proof, easy-to-maintain systems, and must be well aligned with business requirements.

Siebert's background story

Siebert studied Computer Engineering at the University of Pretoria, South Africa and has been working in IT for the last 10 years. He gets excited about all things related to software development although he has a particularly keen interest in software security.

He currently holds the Tech Lead role for a development team at realestate.com.au in Melbourne, Australia.

The External Face – Liz Douglass

Does the role of Tech Lead hold any surprises?

The external-facing aspect of my role is noticeably different from what I've done before. As well as keeping an eye on what's happening with each developer and trying to anticipate what's coming up within the team, I've found that I need to keep a regular dialogue going with the teams that we partner with. This includes both IT groups such as infrastructure, BAU (business as usual), architecture, as well as non-IT groups such as Sales and Marketing. Establishing and maintaining good relationships outside the team has been really important for us.

The pros and cons

Overall, I really enjoy the role. I like being able to share ideas with more people and work through how we can achieve the biggest and fastest. I enjoy grabbing a whiteboard marker and facilitating discussions about what we're doing and how we might progress.

That said, I don't think I've yet mastered the ability

to delegate and I often find myself with too much on my plate. I really dislike leaving my pair when we're ankle-deep in a story. I also think playing two roles has a negative impact on the team because I'm not around all the time.

Any preparation advice?

I am not sure that I could have been better prepared. You never know in advance what you're getting into, and that's one of the best parts of what we do as consultants. In years gone by I have been concerned about needing to 'know everything' in order to be a Tech Lead, which, of course, is a fallacy. Surrounding yourself with people who have different experiences and ideas is the key to being able to cope with anything that comes up.

Where do you go for support?

I think I've been quite fortunate to have always had an amazing support network around me. On this project we have a terrific team, including a project manager who expertly manages the external stakeholders. We also have an excellent business analyst, who is really invested in the client and is a great facilitator and negotiator.

I also have the support of Scott Shaw, a senior technologist, who comes one day per month to visit the team and gives us advice on architecture and technologies.

Has your perspective changed?

I am probably more attuned now to the broader context of the team and the client organisation. I am now even more of an advocate of getting out of your chair and speaking to others - it can save a lot of time and it always leads to better outcomes for everyone.

Liz's background story

Liz started her career with a radically different background, firstly graduating from University as an aerospace engineer from the Royal Melbourne Institute of Technology. She worked for a couple of different aerospace companies which first brought her into contact with software engineers and she learned about build scripts, unit tests and other software development practices.

She joined ThoughtWorks as a developer and has worked in several countries with different teams and roles. In her current role (at the time of this interview) she plays both the role of Tech Lead and Client Principal in building a replacement and refresh of a client's online presence.

> *Editor's note: The Client Principal is responsible for building and maintaining relationships with customers.*

Chaos and Cluelessness – Roy Osherove

Does the role of Tech Lead hold any surprises?

On my first Tech Lead role, what surprised me the most was just how little everyone else around me knew: as little as me. Whatever questions I've had, I've received either incomplete or just horrible answers from people whom I looked up to in other leadership roles.

For example: 'What are we supposed to do with the customer meeting?' and 'How do we work out the requirements?'. It seemed that everyone around me was winging it as much as I was.

The pros and cons

The fact that there was chaos and cluelessness around me was actually a good thing. It allowed someone like me, with a little determination and a little audacity, to do what I needed, wanted, and felt was best for my team. People would ask me, 'Are we there yet?' or ask me to finish things in half the time actually needed to accomplish them, but ultimately I was the one dictating the progress and quality of the project. This is great if you want the chance to experiment with different techniques in a relatively risk-free environment. That particular project was heading for failure anyway, so I tried to at least do it with some test-driven development built in, even though that takes time to learn.

Any preparation advice?

I would have loved someone to tell me how to respond when asked for unreasonable things. My usual reaction was, 'Well... we'll try.' I don't do that any more, but someone should have told me it was my job to *do my job* and not roll over and accept unacceptable requests.

Where do you go for support?

I read The Mythical Man Month and Test Driven Development by Example. I kept reading more and more books and realised everyone has a different opinion, and nobody really knows what's really going on. Years later, a friend told me, 'There are no experts, there is only us.' He was right.

Roy's background story

Roy was born and raised in Israeli. He is the author of The Art of Unit Testing and Notes to a Software Team Leader and has worked with technology for more than 15 years.

He is currently a senior developer/coach/architect in a team working on a government project in Norway.

More Than Just Tech – Priyank Gupta

My view of the Tech Lead role

I believe the Tech Lead is responsible for:

- *The Architecture and Technical Solution* - We worked for a small company that was on a mission to reduce paper and we spearheaded the idea of digital filing cabinets. The appetite for internal hosting and infrastructure was low and the need to innovate was pressing. As part of that we came up with a digital ecosystem in the cloud to help end customers access documents ubiquitously and securely on all sorts of platforms and devices. From the outset, my role was to collaborate, guide, and suggest a suitable technical architecture for the system. It involved reasoning and research to find a suitable technology to provide balance between speed of development and scalability. The anticipated number of end users in the first year of launch was in the hundreds of thousands.

In addition, I focused on designing the API, the web platform design and infrastructure, and the deployment process.

- *Representing the offshore presence* - As I was onshore, closer to the client, one of my main responsibilities was to liaise with, and on behalf of, the offshore team. I voiced their concerns and issues to the technical folk onshore and ensured that everyone was on same page. I relayed any important occurrences back to the offshore contingent; any changes in priority and the technical impacts back and forth. I did this for a combined period of about six months on the project.
- *Coordinating across team roles* - We were one of the core teams working on the product and had several other teams working alongside us: desktop API consumers; mobile app developers; e-commerce platform team, etc. My day-to-day job entailed interacting with them to troubleshoot API issues, looking at design problems from consumer perspectives, and co-ordinating development of API and features that consumers relied on. This gave me the opportunity to analyse all the relevant stories, since tech know-how was required to detail them out.

- *Mediating decisions* - Being in an opinionated team is a great learning opportunity, but it can mean that developer huddles go on for ever, due to divided opinions. One of the roles I assumed was to collate the ideas and bring everyone to an agreement, either by forcing decisions or weighing up business context, needs, and trade-offs. So, while we worked in a fairly rational and democratic way, I was required to take a stand and agree on an approach.
- *Developing* - For most of the time, I was a developer on the team and this was my favourite part. I developed user stories, but I rarely drove them to completion, relying on my pair for that. I rotated frequently to switch context and gain an overall idea of the approach our team was taking on different aspects. This helped me to connect the dots in different discussions with the other developers.

Does the role of Tech Lead hold any surprises?

A couple of surprises stand out for me; the biggest was that most of the issues I had to deal with were less about technology and more about people. I had to balance the needs and aspirations of the team with business needs, to make technical recommendations or push back on certain technology choices. Being exposed to concerns from both the business and developers shifted my perspective from being focused solely on technology to considering the business impact as well. By the end of the project, business drivers had become the central consideration in making decisions.

Another surprise was the need to learn how well motivated my team was. I did this by talking to the team regularly, building rapport with individuals, and finding out about their individual strengths and aspirations. I think this made me a better team player and us a better team. While I have always acknowledged the importance of a closely knit team, this gave me first-hand experience of what goes into proactively building one. The great part was that, although we were distributed, co-sourced (ThoughtWorks and the client's developers), and most of us had never worked with anyone else before, the specific things we organised to build rapport worked really well. This turned out to be my favourite team of my last four years at ThoughtWorks.

On the downside, I hated my inability to form an opinion on certain matters. As a developer, I had had the luxury of not taking part in a discussion if I did not have an opinion. As Tech Lead, people looked to me to drive, mediate, and facilitate discussion, and this was much harder if I didn't have an opinion. It surprised me how, suddenly, it was very important to have an opinion: to defend or argue against crucial bits that would shape the project architecture. I spent considerable time on this: building knowledge to help me form an informed opinion; questioning and reasoning in other subject areas, where depth of knowledge wasn't the root cause.

The pros and cons

I love coding. I love being immersed in a piece of code and taking it to completion. But as Tech Lead I had to get some context on almost all parts of the code so that I could participate in a variety of discussions without getting lost. This meant I had to rotate frequently, which took me away from components I would have loved to spend time working on.

Another key responsibility of the Tech Lead is to 'unblock' people. I would love to say that I worked on this, but in truth, our team was full of extremely competent developers and we never ran out of ideas. So, while I could have done more in this regard, it wasn't really necessary.

One aspect of the role that I really hated was carrying out exercises to provide the business side with a sense of progress. Exercises such as Crystal Ball (a statistical representation where we talked about story completion in terms of days); velocity rationalisation when we were underachieving our target velocity. We soon realised the perils of these discussions and tried to focus on the long-term importance of a feature completion instead of metrics, but it was tricky to the business on side.

On the other hand, there were things that I loved: I learned that understanding each person's technical aspirations helps you manage team dynamics. A person may crave opportunities but may hesitate to proactively take them on. To be able to do this well, I had regular one-on-one talks to get feedback and each person's perspective. While I am not sure how successful I was in my initial intent, it definitely made me connect better to the whole team. I also felt confident of our collective abilities because I had a better sense of individual strengths in the group.

Any preparation advice?

For a distributed team, one of the biggest challenges is overcoming the lack of face time with the customer and the team on the other shore. The rapport and level of trust builds quicker and better when a team is co-located. There are a couple of instances that I can recall, where I would have been more successful if the team had been co-located to start with. I'll try to substantiate with my memory of the experience.

I had the opportunity to work with the client in

their office for the first two months of the project. This was great: I was able to build rapport; I had the trust of the onshore team, and I took that back to offshore. We rotated with everyone to propagate this trust across the team and it worked well. A few months into the project, the client started a small stream of development, staffed entirely by onshore people. None of us had worked with anyone from that stream before. We shared a single codebase. Since we interacted only over the phone, it was harder to push back or talk at length to ensure we were on the same page regarding the architecture.

Because we had separate stand-ups, the lack of day-to-day interaction pushed us into silos. We eventually started to make conflicting decisions. I had another opportunity to work onshore again and I had face time with the other team. Daily interactions made us gel better and had a positive impact on our relationship so that when I worked remotely again, we had a shared understanding and better rapport. We were able to streamline our discussions better, and we better understood each other's concerns.

By the end of the project, the key lesson I had learned was to ensure that a core team works together for a jumpstart period before splitting into smaller, distributed sub-teams. Spending time together in the same location builds mutual trust and confidence.

Trust and confidence, in turn, makes discussions more productive, whether face to face or over the phone. If we had done this earlier, we could have avoided a lot of pain.

Where do you go for support?

I draw support from different places, depending on what sort of challenge I have to face.

With technical challenges, such as validating solutions that the team proposes or more industry-wide accepted solutions, I seek help from the following places:

- Meet-ups and discussions in my local community. Attending specific events related to the technical challenge is a good place to start.
- I ask for opinions and suggestions from external tool or technology communities as well as internal, software-related discussion forums.

I try to widen my perspective on technology by:

- Reading 20 minutes of aggregated content at the start of the day such as HackerNews[6]; Ruby Weekly[7]; Zite[8], or Flipboard[9]. I mark interesting

---

[6] https://news.ycombinator.com/
[7] http://rubyweekly.com/
[8] http://www.zite.com/
[9] https://flipboard.com/

bits for reading later using Pocket[10] and I sift through the content when I have more time during the week.
- I email the most interesting articles to the team, marking them as "Developer Spam". I often receive counter-arguments and different perspectives on the articles I send out.
- I read books and articles on subjects where I want to develop a deeper understanding.

As a Tech Lead, you sometimes have to deliver bad news or push back at non-technical people who put pressure on the team. In the offshore setting, consulting with the client is restricted by the modes of communication available. While video calls are a great way to discuss and thrash out issues, they are not always possible. One key area where I fall short is in pushing back when I don't agree with something (usually technical aspects). I avoid emails to start the discussion, because batting things back and forth tends to leave the crucial discussion in limbo. During a phone discussion, I find I don't get chance to emphasise my point. When I can't discuss my point with the intended parties, I approach onshore team members to convey my opinion and they helped relay it to the customer developer community. My support

---

[10] http://getpocket.com/

network in this area is limited and I reached out only to people I know do this well or, specifically, my sponsor.

Has your perspective changed?

Given that there is no golden scroll handed down from generation to generation, spelling out the responsibilities of Tech Lead, the notions I had about my responsibilities were gleaned from observations of other Tech Leads. One of these was that it was up to me to ensure that we wrote quality code as a team. And when I set out to achieve that, I fell flat on my face due to the sheer overwhelming nature of the task. I did learn a few things as a result.

At the start of every day, I spent 30 minutes browsing through the git commits of the whole team, looking for areas of improvement. It started well, but as we geared up developer pairs and ran full throttle, it became almost impossible to retain all context and contribute to everything objectively. However, one of the ways I started was to comment on a git commit on a specific piece of code to get better insights. This soon became the norm for everyone on the project: everyone looked through commits everyday, asked questions and suggested improvements. This behaviour became viral and we managed to maintain it, even when people rolled off or rolled on, and it automatically improved the overall quality. A similar learning process developed in "Lunch and Learn" sessions, which helped us to improve on pieces of code and technologies that we didn't all know well.

> "Lunch and Learn" sessions are sometimes called "Brown Bag" sessions, where the team has lunch with a discussion around a focused topic, or presentation. These sessions enable rapid learning or exploration in a relatively casual atmosphere.

By the end I had experienced how the role of a Tech Lead was more about facilitating the team and everything else fell into place as a side effect. If I had appreciated that to start with, I would have focused on the right bits.

Also, as I said earlier, the sheer quantity of non-technical work and the priority that business has to take in every decision changed my perspective of the role of Tech Lead.

Priyank's key question: What is required from the Tech Lead of a distributed team?

I am still learning how to deal with being distributed, but I think the key factors are communication and building rapport. A lot of technical capabilities aren't seen or perceived across the shore if you work in isolation or don't communicate well. To maintain effective communications, I have had to step up and take ownership of actionable things that weren't part of my day-to-day work or planned iteration, purely to show willingness to connect and contribute. This gets the relationship between the internal and external team off on the right foot and goes a long way to being successful, despite the distances.

Priyank's background story

Priyank started in the industry in 2004 after graduating with an Engineering degree majoring in Information Technology. He has mostly worked in an offshore context with most of his teams working in a distributed manner. He has worked for clients in a wide range of industries including retail, warranty, and travel and enjoys learning about different domains.

He recently played the Tech Lead role for the first time for a team of approximately 20 people distributed across the US and India.

The Bigger Picture – Suchit Puri

Does the role of Tech Lead hold any surprises?

As a developer, I found most of my focus was on completing a feature in the best possible way. I was concerned with the right design and maintaining an appropriate level of automated test coverage.

As I gained more experience, my focus shifted to the overall design of an application; now I have to consider how the application fits into the whole ecosystem of applications.

As a Tech Lead you have more chance to participate in activities beyond development such as a project initiation, meetings to talk about upcoming business priorities, and earlier opportunities to champion a technical solution.

I feel a Tech Lead has to balance interactions with the business with maintaining a consistent technical direction in the team. Maintaining this balance is even more important in an offshore project because communication channels are limited when people are distributed.

The pros and cons

The thing that I like most about the Tech Lead role is that you get the chance to design complex systems, solve interesting business problems, and still develop well-designed code. I feel writing code is an essential part of being a Tech Lead because there are certain lessons you learn only when you are working with the team on a codebase.

Another great thing about this role is you get more opportunity to interact with the client. I find having more interaction with the client creates better insights for solving and improving business and technical problems. In an offshore project it can be challenging to communicate technical and business solutions, but it is critical to success.

The only thing I don't like about the Tech Lead role is spending lots of times in meetings. Coming from a purely technical background, it took a while for me to adjust to that, because time management is not a skill you practice much as a developer.

Any preparation advice?

I am not sure there is anything you can do to prepare really, as the opportunities in ThoughtWorks are dynamic and extremely contextual. The only skill I learned on the job was to focus energies on the right areas of my project.

I could have spent more time learning about architecting systems end to end.

Where do you go for support?

Discussions in tech forums, office groups, and tech meet-ups gave me a lot of confidence. Casual meet-ups around technology taught me a lot. I met many experienced developers, and I found their experiences with technology especially informative and exciting.

Has your perspective changed?

I think there is a lot of more responsibility on your shoulders when you step into the Tech Lead role. You feel more accountable for the overall design, code quality, testability, and other aspects of the project.

I certainly think more about the future now, particularly designing solutions aimed at the end goal instead of some intermediate one.

I am constantly looking for new technology, approaches and ideas to make your life and your team's life easier.

Suchit's key question: How much project management knowledge should a Tech Lead have?

With our current hiring rate, I find myself with a lot of graduate developers and business analysts. I find myself in many situations where the client asks many questions about story points, velocity, and progress. In situations like this, I feel understanding project management concepts are critical to building a strong relationship with the client.

Suchit's background story

Suchit has worked as an application developer for about five years, starting with a telecommunications company building an application to route calls for call-centre agents. Since then, he has worked with a product company and currently works as a consultant for ThoughtWorks. His most recent team is made up of 12 people, of whom eight are developers and he has played the Tech Lead for this team for almost a year.

Less Coding, More Responsibility – David 'Bucky' Schwarz

Does the role of Tech Lead hold any surprises?

The thing that surprised me most was how much less code I write, even as someone transitioning into a Tech Lead role. I'm spending a lot more time helping other people with their problems, planning, and helping with the overall design of software. One day, a developer that I respect asked me to help him with the backend design of a new feature. It came as a huge surprise to realise that senior developers might look to me for technical help. It hadn't really sunk in until that moment that I was ultimately making the final decisions.

The pros and cons

I like having a direct influence on the development style, tasks, and direction of a particular project. I enjoy mentoring junior team members, and provide knowledge and help when needed; it is good to be able to share knowledge gained through experience and dumb mistakes I've made in the past. I like that my teammates can depend on me to take care of things they need taken care of. I like that I can filter and distil down many disparate remarks and ideas into the essential pieces needed.

What I dislike is that my influence over the direction of the project is no longer expressed through the code I write. I spend more time in meetings than I would like, often listening to people say the same things over and over again. I sometimes find it difficult to watch a junior member struggle and fail at a task that I could finish in a fraction of the time, but I can't intervene because they need to learn from their mistakes.

Any preparation advice?

I think that spending more time mentoring junior members would have better prepared me for the role. I feel that there is a vast difference between the most prolific coder on my team and the least. Dealing with the most prolific is simple and enjoyable, while dealing with the least prolific requires much patience and coaching.

I would also have liked more practice at saying no to people. It's hard when someone is passionate about their job and depending on you to deliver what they want, but real-world constraints force you to tell them no.

Where do you go for support?

My manager has been a good source of support and inspiration. He's one of the best managers I've ever worked for, and he's been coaching me along the way. I enjoy reading Rands in Repose[11] as a way to consolidate my thoughts, and as a source of new ideas and new ways of looking at issues. My manager has recommended a few books on managing software developers. These include:

- Managing Humans: Biting and Humorous Tales of a Software Engineering Manager
- Carrots and Sticks: Unlock the Power of Incentives to Get Things Done
- Target Risk 2: A New Psychology of Safety and Health
- Agile Estimating and Planning
- Planning Extreme Programming
- Blink: The Power of Thinking without Thinking

I always try to store away situations that deeply affected me, both positively and negatively.

Has your perspective changed?

My father has been coaching me in the perspective of managers since I started work. I feel that I've

---

[11] http://www.randsinrepose.com/

understood that there is a lot more going on than my manager lets on, but I never understood just how much until I moved into a greater leadership role. I've learned that most people don't communicate as well as they think they do. I now understand why managers will swing by and ask what's going on, and how (usually) it shouldn't be regarded as antagonistic. My view of how complex an organisation is has changed dramatically. I never fully appreciated how difficult it is to balance dozens of people's competing requests, much less hundreds.

Bucky's key question: Are you happy being a Tech Lead or would you prefer a different role?

Yes, I'm happy being a Tech Lead. I enjoy being in a leadership position even though it was tiring, stressful and nerve-wracking to start with.

Bucky's background story

Bucky started playing around with websites (Flash!) when he was 17 years old, learning as he went. He graduated college with a degree in Computer Science and has been programming professionally for about seven years. He is a Software Engineer on a team of ten that builds email-marketing software for Etsy internal use and is transitioning into the Tech Lead position.

Lean on Communication Skills – Stefan Marev

How do you see your role?

I often find myself communicating the product vision to the teams, because I have been with the company for a long time, have extensive domain knowledge, and spend a lot of time with product managers and directors. As a result, I also attend many of the domain-modelling sessions our team conducts at a whiteboard - techniques borrowed from Domain-Driven Design: Tackling Complexity in the Heart of Software.

I also steer the technical vision for the projects and lead any necessary architecture changes, such as trying to break a 'big ball of mud' domain model into smaller parts that are better distributed. High quality is key to the success of these projects, so I champion efforts around automated testing and other practices that enable continuous delivery.

> *Editor's note: A big ball of mud is a software system haphazardly structured, sprawling, sloppy, duct-tape and bailing wire,*

spaghetti code jungle. See the paper, "A Big Ball of Mud" by Brian Foote and Joseph Yoder (1997)

Does the role of Tech Lead hold any surprises?

The role is more people-oriented than I expected; what surprised me most was probably how small a part technical skills play. I underestimated the difficulties of working with a distributed team too. When you are a developer it is a lot easier for you to determine how successful you are on a day-to-day basis; it is easier to get feedback because the results of your work are more tangible.

The other surprising thing for me was the importance of chemistry - how people fit together in a team - again technical skills are not the only factor. Keeping team morale high at all times can be quite challenging and, more importantly, you are responsible for finding the drivers of each individual team member and looking after their career aspirations.

To begin with, I had to focus a lot more on mentoring, successfully communicating ideas and making the most of each team member. I took a lot for granted while working with people from ThoughtWorks. For example, I had to make the team care about unit testing and mentor test-driven development (TDD) skills - something I'd never thought could take so much effort. I suppose I thought that every developer was more or less the same, but my view on that was one-sided and limited to myself!

The pros and cons

What I like most about the role is that it is challenging, but in a different way from the developer role. It requires me to learn and practice different skills. Mentoring and leadership require good communication skills. I learned a lot about the importance of listening and being patient, skills that are even more requisite when working with a team of less experienced people. I gain a lot of satisfaction from seeing the team become self-organising under my leadership.

I also enjoy the technical challenges of the role as well, such as nurturing and communicating ideas, which I often borrow from reading and following great technical minds online and going to technical meet-ups and talks. The training organisation, SkillsMatter[12] hosts many of these.

What I dislike about the role is having less time for development. I often start developing and pairing with other team members, but I can't see things through and have to leave them to the team to finish. I am naturally pulled into more meetings and have

---

[12]http://skillsmatter.co.uk

to communicate back to high-level managers, which leaves me less time for coding. I miss the time where I can code for days uninterrupted.

The other aspect of the role I don't like is protecting the team from organisational and political issues within the company. For example, having arguments with ivory-tower architects, having to persuade them of the benefits of pair programming and explain that it is not a waste of time. Another frustration is time spent convincing managers that enterprise-ready technologies are not always the best solution. I do understand how important this part of the Tech Lead role is, however, and team morale stays high as a result.

Any preparation advice?

I would have been better prepared for the role if I had taken more initiative as a developer. I spent most of my time coding and focusing on the quality of the code; I think I should have exercised my communication skills. I could have asked to lead retrospectives or facilitate discussions and whiteboard sessions, for example, instead of just taking part and concentrating only on things that were part of the stories and features that I was working on.

On-boarding new team members might have helped me develop as a Tech Lead as well. When I was a developer, I saw that task as boring and repetitive, but now I realise it develops better communication skills. Even though I found myself explaining the same details over and over again, I could have taken the task more seriously and as an opportunity and challenge to improve communicating all dimensions of the project.

In this respect, pair programming is the practice that most helped me to prepare for being a Tech Lead. I found it a great help when preparing to be a Tech Lead to have someone beside me to challenge or confirm ideas and give instant feedback.

Where do you go for support?

I liked the way that my ThoughtWorks teammates had sponsors for every role. The company I work for is not a technology company and application development is a relatively small part of IT, so we don't have the same kind of setup; there are no technical people I can look up to so I draw support from my personal contacts instead. I share ideas and problems with them to get early feedback and help to resolve issues.

At the same time, I have earned the trust of high-level management in my workplace and they give me the time and support to implement new ideas, try out new developer practices and event allowed me to build my own team. I like to think that we've created and work as a small start-up within an enterprise.

The Internet and social networking play an important job for me. I find Twitter an amazing tool for learning from the greatest minds in our industry.

I believe in continuous improvement and strive to get feedback from as many sources as possible. I often ask various people I work with both within and outside the team for feedback.

Any preparation advice?

I recommend you take more initiative, and make the most of every situation and not focus only on coding. I would try to participate in as many diverse tasks as possible to develop different skills. When I was a developer, for example, I really focused on coding tests, features and a tiny bit of build-scripting. I realise now that having more exposure to path-to-production and operations tasks would have helped too.

Stefan's key question: How do you balance your time and ensure you stay hands-on?

This will vary from company to company, but in a traditional IT department like the one in my company, I can tell you it is not an easy job. I do it through prioritisation. I prioritise time for coding and time spent with the team above going to meetings or writing reports, etc. even for the Chief Information Officer (CIO).

I try to avoid becoming the single point of contact for technical concerns on the project. I create champions within the teams and ask them to communicate solutions both within and outside the team. I don't know how successful I am at this, but I keep trying! I'd like to find more sources for advice on this. I have found a lot of good advice on communicating goals within the team, but less on communicating technical ideas effectively to the rest of the organisation.

Stefan's background story

Stefan has worked in technology since 2005 and has worked with web technologies since at the University of Westminster and Reed Business Information (RBI) in the United Kingdom. He joined GroupM where he helps build web-based systems for media planning and buying.

Stefan has always had a passion for agile methodologies and engineering practices and was influenced greatly by working with a team of consultants from ThoughtWorks. He is currently leading three small teams, two of which are near-shore where he works closely with a second Tech Lead to provide continuity when he rotates to a different team.

Practitioners

> *"Wisdom comes from experience. Experience is often a result of lack of wisdom."*
> - Terry Pratchett

For this section I interviewed Tech Leads who have worked in the role for a number of years or across a number of teams. I asked them to share their own stories, the challenges they faced, and the wisdom they found over time. They share their experiences across a wide range of industries, a wide range of team sizes and, as a result, a wide range of lessons learned.

With a role split across several dimensions, effective time-management becomes even more important, so I asked each person to share their own approach. They describe where to find time, how to identify tasks, strategies for delegation and, most importantly, how to maintain the delicate balance of heads-down time in code and juggling their other responsibilities.

I grouped their responses into four themes:

1. People
2. The Tech of a Tech Lead
3. Bridging Business with Tech
4. You

I feel these four themes represent different facets of the Tech Lead role, and resonate strongly with the responses from different people. I provide a brief commentary for each of these themes, summarising people's responses and adding observations from my own experience as a Tech Lead.

People

People and teams are inextricably linked. A team does not exist without people, and it takes effort to turn a set of people into a team.

> *"A set of people does not make a team. It only exists as a group. A team is a set of people working towards a common goal. An effective leader aligns people towards that goal."* - Anonymous

Remaining Technically Grounded

When a developer first moves into the role of Tech Lead, their focus will be almost exclusively on the technical aspects. Some developers interpret the Tech Lead role as being the final decision maker on difficult technical choices or as focusing on the most technically difficult problem.

These interviews reveal a very different take. Yes, a Tech Lead must be technically competent, since this helps build respect and rapport with people, however the Tech Lead does not necessarily need to be the best technically and, in many cases, does not necessarily have the deepest technical skills on the team.

Finding and Developing Good People

No one sets out to find mediocre people for their team. Every Tech Lead will say they hire good people. Tech Leads are naturally part of the interview process, looking for cultural fit, aptitude, and a positive attitude to learning. However, finding the ideal candidate in a timely fashion is difficult in today's dynamic labour market.

In addition to finding good people, the effective Tech Lead focuses equally on growing developers in their team. A common practice is to meet one-on-one with each developer to find out what their interests are, what motivates them and what they consider their strengths to be. With this information, the Tech Lead constantly seeks ways to match interests and opportunities across the team. One interviewee in this section talks about appreciating the mix of skills and experience as a team strength.

For example, a task may be perceived trivial by one person because they have worked on many similar problems in the past. For another person, this same task could be extremely interesting because it is a new type of problem for them to solve.

Keeping track of what people find interesting evolves over time as people grow, and learn. The only way a Tech Lead can keep up with these changes is to ask people frequently enough.

A Tech Lead grows developers by encouraging them to step outside of "just programming" and work closely with other people in the software development process. Developers working more closely with testers build a better understanding of what it takes to make more robust code. Developers working more closely with end-users and business stakeholders better understand what acceptable trade-offs may be made and the real problem that needs solving.

Listening to the Team

The Tech Lead finds opportunities to listen to the people on their team. One Tech Lead asks: "Is my team set up as well as it can be?" When starting with a new team, I ask myself, "Does everyone feel comfortable expressing their opinion?" Tech Leads need to establish safety.

Once you create safety you must then cultivate motivation for full team effectiveness. Different things motivate different people and it takes time to find out what each person wants to do and find opportunities to do them. Listening is the key to this.

Tech Leads spend less time in code, so they rely more heavily on information from the team. Drawing factual information out of developers can be difficult because developers habitually present solutions to problems and opinions rather than facts. You draw upon good questioning skills to draw out the information you need to make better decisions.

Appreciating Individual Strengths

A Tech Lead appreciates the different strengths that each person brings to the team. Over time you will recognise these different strengths. For example, some developers are better thinking in more abstract terms, whilst others are more detail-oriented. Some developers will be better thinking visually, whilst others must communicate best through code.

Differences in strengths bring opportunities for learning and better problem solving but they also create an opportunity for conflict. The Tech Lead pays attention to heated discussions in the team and helps the team move forward when too much conflict threatens to permanently damage team relationships. Tech Leads should not be afraid to facilitate technical discussions (particularly heated ones!) in order to move forward. Very rarely will a Tech Lead step in to override a decision as this disempowers team members and generates resentment.

Team Focus – Alison Rosewarne

What should a Tech Lead focus on and why?

Team focus: it is important that the team can actually focus and knows what is important. This enables good decision-making and ensures good results. Different teams have different needs and different obstacles to overcome to achieve focus.

I worry about team engagement and want everyone to be challenged with the work that they do. Spending time on 1-to-1s is generally the best way to gauge interest and enthusiasm.

What has been your biggest challenge as a Tech Lead?

Working with an offshore development team in an agile manner has been the most challenging situation I've experienced as a Tech Lead. It is easy to take corridor conversations for granted; it is easier to absorb incidental context when everyone is co-located, working in the same environment.

Handling a distributed team requires constant awareness of the situation. More time is needed to ensure the remote team is kept up to speed with decisions made locally and you need to use whatever technology is available to decrease the distance and improve communication bandwidth. Ad hoc communication tools such as Skype are better than email or after-the-fact documentation.

Any time-management tips?

I am a dedicated list maker. Each week I review the priorities and plan at least three things that I want to achieve each day. It is important to understand competing priorities so any interruptions can be managed. Some work has to be done (deferring planned tasks), while other work can be deferred. I keep track of unexpected work for later review. Occasionally booking time in my calendar or working from home is necessary to ensure tasks requiring focus can be completed without interruption.

How do you strike the right balance between writing code and dealing with other issues?

I don't write as much code as I would like to; the split between writing code myself and doing other things is about 20/80. This can change depending on what stage a project is at. I have had to accept that it is more productive to pair with team members and provide guidance about the code they produce rather than writing all the code myself.

Alison's key question: What skill helps most with tech leadership?

The ability to delegate and good communication skills are essential to technical leadership. Of these two, I would say good communication skills are the most helpful. As a Tech Lead you need to tailor your communication for both technical and non-technical audiences.

For technical audiences you need to know what you are talking about; you cannot fake it, as people can tell. It is important to summarise detail and achieve consensus amongst the group. For non-technical audiences you need to translate the effort involved in different approaches and trade-offs to gain support for architectural choices and spending time on technical activities such as effort in reducing technical debt.

Alison's background story

Alison has worked as Tech Lead for the Commercial team at REA Group for two years. She started working in the IT industry after graduating from RMIT University in Melbourne, Australia. For the last ten years she has worked across many industries such as gaming, superannuation, defence, and insurance.

She has lead technical teams on and off over the last six years depending on the consulting engagement. Her core development experiences were in Java/J2EE and more recently she has been developing with Ruby and associated web frameworks.

Team over Self – Humphrey Elton

What should a Tech Lead should focus on and why?

I expect to lead people who are professional without pretensions. I do not expect to oversee all code. I do, however, expect teams to work together. For me, a developer's skills with personal relationships and communication are as important as code writing, possibly more so. A mix of abilities in the team means that the guns have to help junior developers and give them space to learn themselves. I have fewer issues with simplistic, and even inefficient code.

In my area of software development, memory is cheap, CPU is cheap and complex code is too costly to maintain, so do not ask me to write a disk subsystem!

I try to keep an ear out for the noise coming from any team. At one extreme, too much talking might indicate people being too unproductive and that the team are not making decisions, or they might be having just too good a time. At the other extreme, too quiet might mean everyone is heading in their own direction and the code will not combine well, or that there are personality issues brewing.

Discussion is good but unproductive and frustrating for all unless its focus is choosing an outcome.

What has been your most challenging situation as a Tech Lead and how did you handle it?

My most challenging situation was managing a mixed team of some technically very good developers and some juniors. That team had a lot of issues, of which having two different managers was the very least. The team members were completely at odds with each other. Parts of the team had significantly different code styles, because some were Java developers, but a lot of Javascript was required and there was no consistent approach to implementing new features. The "gurus" would also write code, leaving the "unit tests" to the juniors.

We held a meeting, in which I was involved only because one manager was away. We put all known issues on the table and allowed the meeting get to a fragile, but sweet point, where I stopped it. We then gave the team a couple of minutes to resolve each problem, and if they couldn't reach a decision, I would step in to make one. I only had to do a couple; the team worked the rest out.

I ensured that everyone in the team had a say somewhere. There is no one less productive than a junior whose good idea gets ignored, or whose code gets refactored within a week. I only insisted on one item: if it works, then leave it and move on.

What are your secrets to managing time?

As a Tech Lead you want your team to be productive.

Your time is only one person's worth. Your team's is n times that. Your focus should be on their productivity.

Try to find the balance of good team time, while letting each have their own best time. I am most productive late in the afternoon. If people interrupt me then I try to get them to organise a time the next morning.

I have Wednesday afternoons off because of my kids. Management hates it, but it gives the team time to be self-responsible. Sometimes I pick up the kids, then log in remotely and finish stuff, other times not.

You will probably find you cannot choose all the tasks that match your skills, because interruptions mean you can't guarantee they will be completed on time. You just have to be more careful about what you take on.

How do you find the balance writing code and dealing with other issues?

Balancing writing code and dealing with other issues is a constant conflict, and always will be. Interruptions must be dealt with sooner rather than later. If you do not address them, they will stack up and swamp you. I have naughty days when I really just want to code, but I pay for it later. Indulge yourself occasionally!

I try to deal with a lot of the issues myself, but if I can delegate problems or decisions to someone in the team, then I will. I cannot remember when I last overrode what they decided. Their decision may not be the one that I would have made, but it is almost always good enough. Do not do it all; but do not delegate it all either. I try not to have too many rules about what I do versus what I delegate. I try things, make a few mistakes, and learn from them.

Deciding to be a Tech Lead is a step away from coding, unless you are willing to do longer hours or it is really clear that you have no line management. I have never worked that way and do not think that it is possible.

The role involves dealing more with people than I realised. If you do not want to have to deal with people or do not think it is important, then the Tech Lead role may not be for you. You need to actively build relationships and have on eye on the relationships within the team.

I do not get to explore, or try different things in code that I used to do much more as a developer.

Humphrey's key question: Is it a sensible role in an organisation?

Probably not! You are unproductive for your skills. What you can deliver by when is unpredictable. The role is one step away from coding. Whenever you get really focused, someone will come along and interrupt it. You will inevitably get staler in your favourite language, but hopefully you will have the maturity to appreciate that most of the issues are not really language specific.

You have to start reading all management emails more carefully; maybe even start doing it for once! You have to learn to have one ear on the room, while you are trying to concentrate. You also have to decide when to stick your nose into anything. At the same time, you must give your team space and remember how often problems got solved without a Tech Lead or someone else getting involved. You become half management, half grunt. It is not easy as you are inevitably on both sides, yet in neither camp completely.

I imagine this role is like that of a corporal or sergeant in the army. People obey authority, often in the face of complete incompetency, and you must learn when to use it. Find the style of your inner tinpot tyrant. Use it wisely.

Inevitably you are managing the team. You need to decide what the team should decide for themselves. It would be an understatememt to say I really hate code style discussions, for example, so I let the team choose! They have to live in it more than you, but only give them two minutes to discuss it! It can go on for much longer, but you always have veto!

Humphrey's background story

Humphrey considers himself less of a "technical" Tech Lead than most despite working in development for 20 years and dealing with technologies such as Fortran, OpenVMS-TPU (Virtual Memory System-Text Processing Utility). He has more recently worked with Java, Flex, PHP and Python.

Delegate, Delegate, Delegate – Jason Selby

What should a Tech Lead focus on and why?

Team dynamics. Once you stop focusing on being an individual contributor, the health of the team culture is the most valuable area that the Tech Lead can greatly influence and directly affects team performance. There are many things the Tech Lead can do to impact culture and dynamics. You can identify and address internal and external conflicts early, coach individuals on technical and behavioural improvements, and clear roadblocks to keep the team from spinning on external constraints.

What has been your biggest challenge as a Tech Lead?

One of my guiding principles is for key decisions to be delegated to the team as frequently as possible. This is often impossible when dealing with personnel issues, but otherwise it works well. Letting the team own decisions ensures buy-in, both on approach and ownership of outcomes at a team level, especially when things don't go exactly as planned.

Although the principle is sound, it isn't always easy to adhere to in practice.

When I was leading a team at a large consumer electronics retailer, for example, we were discussing the design of a service endpoint. This particular service would not be called every time a web page was rendered, but our traffic model projected that the endpoint would see traffic about 50% of the time. At the retailer's operating scale, this was still a substantial quantity of traffic.

Of the two leading designs, one was a more compute-intensive solution with less development time and one was quite a bit more development work, but would require almost no computation at request time. I favoured the solution that took more development time but guaranteed production performance. A number of senior members of the team wanted to proceed with the solution that optimised for development time; they were willing to take the performance risk in order to have more time to focus on other development work that was also critical to be completed prior to the rush of holiday traffic.

After some debate, we put it to a vote and based on a slight majority, went with the compute-intensive solution. It was hard for me to accept that my arguments weren't persuasive enough. It was difficult to resist the temptation to overrule the team and impose my solution by fiat. The holiday came and went and the team decision proved right; the compute-intensive solution had been a concern through the holiday period, but it didn't cause any problems, and having additional time to focus on other development priorities meant that we addressed other performance concerns and so probably prevented other performance problems.

Any time-management tips?

I get in early each day, usually an hour before the rest of the team. This allows me time to catch up on administrative tasks and email. With those chores out of the way, I'm more focused when the team starts trickling into the office.

Another major time-consumer is answering questions from other teams. The teams I've led have been agile teams with a strong emphasis on low-ceremony collaboration. This means we encourage other teams we work with to come to our development lab when they have questions or needs. The problem was that, since I was the Tech Lead and the recognisable face of the team, I was interrupted many times a day to answer questions or help draft requests for new features. I solved this by introducing a rotating role of "Concierge" to our team, who was dedicated to answering drop-in requests on a given day. My team is happy to get get better acquainted with our larger community and the interruptions are tolerable since they're spread across all members of the team over a few weeks.

How do you strike the right balance between writing code and dealing with other issues?

I work hard to keep meetings scheduled in contiguous blocks and only on certain days. This allows me to have time to be focused and work with the development team. Making time to be around the team and present is key to effective and authentic leadership.

I'm also merciless about opting out of low-value meetings or those that lack a crisp agenda. This isn't possible in all contexts, but my current employer has a meeting-heavy culture and if I didn't reject a lot of meetings, I would have little time for anything else. This doesn't make me very popular, but I try to be kind when declining. Staying focused allows my team and me to deliver.

There are always enough non-development tasks to fill every single day. Determining which meetings and tasks are optional takes time and a bit of delicate experimentation. I usually attend all meetings and follow through on all tasks at the start of a project and as I get a feel for those that are not adding value, I start to decline them one at a time and watch to see if there are any consequences. If I misjudge the importance, I say I overlooked the meeting or task without substantial impact to my relationships.

Jason's key question: What was the hardest change for you when transitioned from developer to Tech Lead?

I was used to being one of the strongest technical contributors on teams prior to becoming a Tech Lead. Once I took on leadership responsibilities, I was no longer present for all team conversations nor able to be involved in the implementation details of every feature. The team often looked to me to help arbitrate and break contentious deadlocks. I struggled to let go of being involved in the implementation of every feature and driving particular implementation approaches. Had I continued to be outspoken, I would have compromised my ability to arbitrate and tie-break.

Jason's background story

Jason considers himself first as a software developer, even though he has been leading teams for the past six years. His career has focused mostly on high-scale, high-availability systems in business domains such as banking, insurance, utilities and retail.

Facilitating, then Leading – Dan Abel

What should a Tech Lead focus on and why?

People can be the biggest challenge to co-ordinate and inspire, but are the most powerful force to throw at any problem. To know your team and for them to know you allows you to work as a leader, a facilitator, and coach to guide the group to powerful actions.

My guiding rule is to lead where they cannot and to facilitate where they can. That means getting out of their way where they can shine, putting just enough structure around them up to ensure they are supported. And leading from the front where the team needs a strong guide to get on top of a challenge.

When it comes to leadership, I've found it essential to find opportunities to help the team grow so that I have the freedom to just facilitate things I was once leading. To do that I need to be able to observe and judge fairly; looking to the future, listening and directing in equal measure. I've found that in that way you don't have to start with a great team, you can build one.

If you want a point about technical discovery, it's about deciding what might look good and then incrementally working towards that, measuring and assessing, being willing and ready to rip some of it up if we find out we were wrong. Being a leader means managing the risks and last responsible moments to the best of my ability. I find it hard, but I try to work through Plan Do Measure Adjust cycles: just enough, ready in time.

What has been your biggest challenge as a Tech Lead?

I'm allergic to Gantt charts and in-depth project plans, though I love working in partnership with a great project or programme manager. Early on in my career, during the second time I was a Tech Lead, the Project Manager asked me to come up with some rough estimates based on what we knew. He wanted to have a plan to talk through during a meeting. The client took hold of this Gantt chart, simply moving along the plan without revising it based on new information we had learned. The client wasn't interested in adjusting the plan, even after conversations highlighting the risks involved. In the end, I talked to a director and gained his support to change our working style after showing him the risk involved.

Now I might solve the problem differently, but I

would still attack the root cause. I cannot sit back and do nothing if we know about something that will prevent a successful delivery. We should act on what we know, even if it involves bad news and difficult conversations.

A few years later I had to deliver bad news myself. I inherited a project that didn't meet all client expectations. It was my job to solve the problem. I created a table, highlighting the features the client expected and where we were before using that in the conversation with the client. Not talking about the issue would have made things worse. Bad news has to be dealt with and a plan made over what to do next.

Any time-management tips?

Life tends to throw me challenges that are always slightly bigger than I'm ready for Ð or perhaps my eyes are bigger than my belly? The result is that when there is a problem I can be really focused, but when it is business as usual, I have been known to struggle to know what to do next and get everything important done.

Some years ago I read the advice of Rands' on how to do what I see as the urgent[13] and the important[14],

---

[13]http://www.randsinrepose.com/archives/2008/07/22/the_taste_of_the_day.html

[14]http://www.randsinrepose.com/archives/2008/08/18/the_trickle_list.html

which had a big effect on how I worked. The Urgent is the stuff that you need to get done: perhaps people are asking for it; perhaps you have decided it needs to happen. The Important is the stuff that means you wouldn't be doing your job if you ignored it, but no one is asking you to do; this stuff isn't milestones, but it is the flow of your day and your week, your chats to your team members, being sure to pair, what's going on the story wall, are your team happy and satisfied?

Though I don't follow his processes verbatim, I use index cards for my to-do list; Rands' Daily Scrub helped me deal with more work that I could do, and the trickle list helped me focus past that into the zone of rich conversations that seem to catch things I didn't know about. A mixture of this, and short, more formal meetings helps me to intuit what is going on and what might need to get on to my to-do deck.

How do you strike the right balance between writing code and dealing with other issues?

I've not been very good at this recently, but I'm fortunate as I'm often surrounded by good developers who let me drop in and out.

A lot depends on the size and composition of the team: when I've been on a smaller team, it's obvious that I should be spending my time coding; on larger teams, I like the idea of blocking out some core coding hours where I can focus on that part of my job. When I've been involved in multi-team deliveries, I've made a point of spending my limited coding time in pairing on areas where I know there has been pain or a challenge and I want to set the work and the code up for success, giving me a chance to understand the surprises and pressures that might lurk in the area first hand.

I don't want to slip, so this year I'm looking to mix things up a bit and work on projects that allow me to have a more code-facing role.

Dan's key question: When does the Tech Lead role stop and other roles begin?

A Tech Lead finds balance between urgent and important tasks, and between doing and looking forward. When a Tech Lead focuses on one aspect too much, I see them opting out of the role. For example, if I am in meetings all the time, or I am permanently focused on solving a deep technical problem, then my team is missing a Tech Lead.

Dan's background story

Dan started to explore what computers can do at an early age and followed this up by studying both computers in the C programming language and people at college, with the help of dancing and lots of cider. In

18 years, he has seen environments of all types from small start-ups to a large C++ product company.

He has lead teams on several occasions and now recognises what is important: relying on a strong goal, the means to get there and working with people willing to learn.

Helping the Team – Adam Esterline

What should a Tech Lead focus on and why?

I think the most important thing a Tech Lead can do is to help their team figure out what work they are not going to do. Lots of things can occupy a team, such as refactoring, learning new technologies, adding new features, and fixing bugs. Most of the time, we want to do all those things, but we have to learn how to say no. Saying no can come in many forms. For example, saying, "We already have it," or asking, "Is it the most important thing now?".

My biggest worry is probably making sure the team feels like it is successful. Writing code is hard and it is easy to burn out. I try to make sure that the teams are seeing benefits from their work on a regular basis.

What has been your biggest challenge as a Tech Lead?

Two real challenges come to mind. The first one arose when the code the team was working on had got into a bad state. We were having trouble delivering code on a regular basis. As a team, we decided we needed to stop delivering features and work on the code that caused problems. This was not a popular decision with all our stakeholders. We drew up a relatively short list of problems that needed to be addressed and we focused on solving them over the following three months so that we could then get back into a stable state and start delivering features again.

The second challenge I had was deciding to move to continuous deployment; this was a tough team situation that really paid off. There was a lot of fear and uncertainty when deploying every commit. People were asking questions such as, "How does QA fit into this model?" and "Can we really trust developers with that much responsibility?". We spent a lot of time discussing each of these issues. We spent considerable time writing a "safety net" that would allow us to deploy code safely. We also spent time introducing failures into the system to see how our safety net performed. In the end, we built a system that can react quickly to customer needs and issues.

Any time-management tips?

I block out time in my calendar from 8am to 1pm every day, when I will not accept meetings. I use that time to code and work with my team. Where I spend my mornings coding with the team, I use the afternoons dealing with issues. If I do not block off time in my calendar, I would end up spending almost all my time working on issues.

I also make it a point to only answer email first thing in the morning or late at night. I try to check emails only at that time.

Adam's background story

Adam has worked with a wide range of programming languages since 1999 and has spent several years running training classes for Washington University in St. Louis. Adam has lead teams since 2003 in everything from projects involving hardware to high-traffic websites.

Inwards and Outwards – Rachel Laycock

What should a Tech Lead focus on and why?

I think the Tech Lead takes two stances, looking both inwards and outwards.

Inwardly, the most important thing is the team, and the dynamics of the team. I watch for the dynamics of entire team, not just the developers. I watch how the developers interact with other roles in the team such as analysts, testers, and the project manager. I think about whether people are learning, or watch if people are keeping up and, if not, consider what support they need. I find out where a person wants to focus their growth and see if people feel comfortable taking ownership of tasks, championing ideas, and growing. In many ways, I protect the team in the same way a project manager might. I try to shield the technical team from spending too much time in meetings about architecture or ideation of future work, so they can focus on prioritising work in the present.

Outwardly, I often act as the conduit between the

technical team and the business. I consider whether we are meeting stakeholder needs, and whether our solution answers the problem in the best way possible. I ask myself, "Are the right people involved at the right time to make the best possible decisions?" I constantly step back to look at the bigger picture to check the project is heading in the right direction and aligns with future releases. I am also an adviser to project managers and analysts to facilitate good decisions, adding a much-needed technical perspective to the analysis phase.

What has been your biggest challenge as a Tech Lead?

Delegation is something I still struggle with, so I'll exemplify this, but there have been many challenges around stakeholder management and managing expectations, which have been difficult lessons to learn as well.

I was working as a Tech Lead Architect role at a large financial company; I had another consultant from ThoughtWorks with me (some of the time), and a team of client developers. In addition, I needed to manage the executive stakeholders and their constant demands and expectations. I didn't have the usual constructs of BA, PM etc, so I had a lot of gaps to fill. This is where I really struggled with delegation.

I didn't handle it well at first; I just gave people work to do piecemeal and this meant that the developers always had to ask what to do next, just when I was so busy I couldn't think what to give them, or, at least, felt comfortable giving them.

Eventually, I realised I would work myself to death unless I let some stuff go and let them own work and learn how to manage and prioritise their work based on information I gave them. It was hard, but I stopped to ask each of the developers what they actually wanted to learn and work on. One developer wanted to develop better consulting skills, so I let him run meetings and present to the client with my support. I would then give him feedback on specifics of what went well and what they could improve. It was hard for me to let stuff go, but it did change the attitude of the team and I wasn't constantly being asked what to do next.

Delegation is especially hard when you know how to do a task and the other person is still learning. You know they may not do the task as well as you could, but they need to make mistakes in order to learn. The advantage is that you are no longer doing everything!

Any time-management tips?

This ties in with delegation: it is something I am still working on! I am discovering that breaking things down into high-level concepts and then prioritising them is working for me right now. So, for example, I start by deciding what I need to do and then define priorities; I have to be realistic with myself about what I can achieve, given that my calendar is often full of meetings. There will always be tasks I cannot get done, so then I think about who I can delegate those to. I try to base my decision on the areas where people want to grow, but sometimes I simply have to ask them to do tasks they may not care for.

To summarise, I break things down into three or four high-level tasks, prioritise, then delegate. I refer to "Your Brain at Work" (David Rock), which explains that prioritisation and decision-making is hard for the human brain to do, so you should do it when you are at your best and make it easier on yourself by breaking it into three or four things.

It doesn't always work; I often try to do it all myself, but I am constantly working on myself as well as the team.

How do you strike the right balance between writing code and dealing with other issues?

It is hard. Coding is a very focused activity and I can lose myself in a story and become focused on the next test to write, for example, but as a Tech Lead you need to keep an eye on the architecture, the evolution of the code, does it meet the broader goals? Will the solution work with things that are in the pipeline - things that only you may know about because you were in the meeting to talk about the next release. You also need to pay attention to team dynamics. Are the right people pairing with each other? Are people growing? Personally, I find it easier if I drop in and out of stories rather than owning them. Then I don't get too caught up in too much detail and I can remind myself that I am more a coach than a coder for my team.

Rachel's first key question: "How would you coach a developer into being a Tech Lead?"

The most important point is that they understand that they are no longer responsible for being the best coder on the team, but for making sure everyone else does their best. Help them to see the risks involved and help them find ways of encouraging everyone else to contribute, particularly if they are leading an inexperienced team. Show them ways to spread responsibility for designs in the team. Encourage them to use a Socratic questioning method instead of letting them first present their idea to a team. Teach them various questioning styles to help the team come up with the answers themselves. The question, "What about?" often helps.

Teach them to recognise the skills people have and where they might be best applied. Help them to find a balance between sharing skills across the team and being "efficient" with software delivery. Help the developer build listening and influencing skills, as they will have more interaction with the business and potentially other technical teams, architects or other Tech Leads. Finally, identify a support network for the developer and persuade them to not suffer in silence and to ask for help when needed. Help them find a good mentor with more experience, or someone who works in a different role to get feedback on ideas, and to provide support or guidance through trying times.

Rachel's second key question: "How do you remain technical and relevant when you don't get to code that often?" Accept that you are unlikely to remain the best coder on the team, purely because you will be coding less. Focus on what you *need* to know or learn for the context. You must still demonstrate passion about being technical because you may find yourself learning more in your own time.

Encourage the team to organise "Brown bag" sessions to keep you and other team members abreast of what the team is learning. You will rely more on reading the code to understand what is going on and pair-program with developers as much as possible. I aim to make this about 50 per cent of my time.

Rachel's background story

Rachel is a software development veteran of ten years, having led six teams in the past. The role has interested her since she first wore the Tech Lead mantle and discovered people problems are much more difficult to solve than technical ones. She used to think the most technical person on the team should lead, but realised deep technical knowledge does not aid the Tech Lead in solving people problems. Rachel is also particularly passionate about how to get and keep more women in technology, particularly in technologist roles. She would also like to see women play the Tech Lead role more often.

Soft Skills – Jon Pither

What should a Tech Lead focus on and why?

Get the best people in your team. It is such an obvious point, but the best people tend to solve most problems for you. For example, problems of having to educate and line manage can quickly evaporate into questions of how you should best delegate.

I love self-organising teams. At the same time, a Tech Lead needs to bring positive energy. A Tech Lead needs to stir things up, to ask questions, and to facilitate meetings so that everyone can have a fair say. I do this by drawing upon good old-fashioned meeting management techniques, focusing on the biggest issue for the day, and seeking agreement on outcomes. Although some people think well-established teams don't require facilitation, in my experience this is rarely true, especially when the problem is complex or ill defined. It can be exhausting, but a lead must be prepared to give a lot of themselves, emotionally and intellectually.

Tech Leads should focus on developing soft skills.

A good Tech Lead draws upon these skills to seek balance between team members, to push boundaries of what is possible, and to notice those happy to stay within their comfort zone. I should point out that your job as Tech Lead is not to automatically solve or increase friction. Disagreements are healthy as long as it does not block the team from moving forward.

Lastly, a Tech Lead should be prepared to step aside for the greater good, by which I mean finding the right balance between three elements:

- The employers or the business: those who foot the bill ultimately represent the greater good.
- The project: teams come, go, and change over time. The systems we build outlive us.
- The team: I consider the team as individuals first, and as a collective around what would make people happy. I like to quote of a former colleague of mine (Häken Räberg): "We are not paid to enjoy ourselves at work, but it doesn't hurt."

Whoever works in this role should be working in the interests of the team. When a team is undertaking a radical transformation, for example, a change of language and supporting technologies, the Tech Lead role may better be transitioned or shared.

What has been your biggest challenge as a Tech Lead?

I once stepped down from the role of Tech Lead as I felt I had to devote all my energy to coding. I brought the team into a state of near anarchy to facilitate a technology shift and felt someone else could do a better job of restoring some process, cleaning up my mess. I also felt extremely dedicated to ensuring the technology shift succeeded, so this was where I needed to focus my energy. This left little time for other Tech Lead responsibilities that can be emotionally draining on many fronts.

Since I was trying to be an agent for change, I needed someone else to take on the role of calming agent; someone who could better integrate the views of team members with opposing strategies, of which I was one. I could not play both roles. I found a successor who, I believed, had the necessary soft skills to facilitate heated discussions and had the appreciation of the bigger picture.

Another challenge I have often encountered is dealing with a team getting stale. A team needs new blood; it needs new sources of creativity. To do this, I sought out amazing graduates to lift a team, as well as scouring my network for people I highly admire, whom I think should make a difference and excite people.

I find it hard to deal with developers in my team who lean towards a conservative or a negative viewpoint. I want everyone in my team to be happy and excited, but perhaps this is one of my own failings. You need different people on a team with different viewpoints and different strengths. Just because I am a Tech Lead I should not lose sleep over people not being thrilled by work the team is doing.

Any time-management tips?

To-do lists are essential. Boring things like using a calendar help. Org mode in Emacs rocks too.

How do you strike the right balance between writing code and dealing with other issues?

You shouldn't hang on to being a Tech Lead and writing code all the time. If you cannot do both, then don't: pick one. I once read somewhere on a Java forum: "Pick one thing and do it well rather than suck at both."

But I've had great success and joy from delegation. If you have a great team, delegate. Set up "stream leads" or Tech Leads over a smaller area. Ask the team how they feel you can best delegate. Retrospectives are a must. A boozy pub scene doesn't hurt.

Jon's first key question: Do I consider myself a good Tech Lead?

I have mixed feelings about this. I can bring good energy; I can gain a team's trust and be willing to push whatever barrier presents itself. On the other hand, I struggle with my own demons of confidence, of not feeling good enough to lead some amazing people. It can be challenging. I can get stressed when I feel my team is under attack from people in large institutions that may not respect the work we do. I am a very passionate person, and sometimes I feel I would benefit from being more savvy at politics.

Jon's second key question: How can I improve myself?

Meditate every day! Try not to take the work too seriously and enjoy the playfulness inside teams more. I love communication techniques like Nonviolent communication, although it is too easy to forget such practices.

Jon's background story

Jon has worked in IT for 12 years, where he has acted as the Tech Lead for three to four teams in the last four years. He has a particularly strong passion in using and contributing to open source software and has most recently found a passion for using Clojure to solve problems.

Enabling People – Isabella Degen

What should a Tech Lead focus on and why?

A Tech Lead should enable each person on the team to be as productive as they can be. They should make each team member feel they are part of a single team working towards the same goal. They ensure developers truly understand the requirements and co-own the codebase. One way I achieve this is by ensuring I do not present my ideas first, and by encouraging others to share their ideas. I try not to tell people what I would do, because I find this discourages people from presenting their own ideas. I am careful about that, and although it depends on the team, I delay presenting my own ideas until I better know the people on the team.

I try to spend half an hour every day with the developers on the team to ask questions such as:

- What problems exist in the codebase?
- Do you have any new ideas to try?

- Where are we spending the most time and what can we do about it?
- Is there anything on your mind?

I spend a lot of time trying to encourage less experienced developers to share their ideas, because even though they may not always work, they often come up with different approaches. Mixed with the experience of seasoned developers, we often end up with a new solution that will work.

Some ideas take a long time, so I also work with developers to find ways we can incrementally improve to help with the next set of functionality being developed. I find this is the best way for getting stakeholder support for technical improvements.

Tech Leads should also ensure different roles on a project do not work in their own silos, throwing work over a wall. I try to prevent developers picking up work without involving other roles and, if I notice it, will often send the Business Analyst (BA) and Quality Analyst (QA) their way. What I find interesting is that BAs and QAs, who are normally the minority of the team, never have issues involving other roles. They want to talk. It is often developers, who think they know what needs to be done, who need the encouragement to work with people in other roles.

Another way I try to break silos across teams is often at social events. As a Tech Lead, I often spend more time with people in the roles of Project Manager or Product Owner. At social occasions such as a team lunch, I try to avoid sitting next to these people to give others an opportunity to interact with them.

A Tech Lead should focus on the *path to production*. I like to start designing and architecting a solution by envisaging a go-live date, the release into production, and work backwards from there. I identify what work must be done, and the impediments we might encounter and must overcome.

A Tech Lead works with the business to develop a shared understanding of how much work can be done, and therefore help prioritising what they want to do. They also help non-technical team members understand what is occurring in the development team by translating technical needs and terms into a more general language.

What has been your most challenging situation as a Tech Lead and how did you handle it?

My first project as Tech Lead was the most challenging situation, because I did not have the experience and did not understand what the role was about. I found it difficult to get the team to respect me, which, in hindsight, is no surprise given that I totally misunderstood that I had to give the team the freedom to design their work. I should have been acting as a shepherd, looking after them and steering them loosely in the right direction, rather than enforcing all my ideas.

Luckily, I was working with an experienced project manager and we spent an hour together every day to discuss problems. These discussions helped me understand more about my role. Feedback from all the team members was what made me change my approach the next time round and ever since.

Any time-management tips?

Every day, before our team's stand-up meeting, I try to arrive early so that I can spend 40 minutes in total quiet where I can ponder over what is going on in the project. I ask myself questions like, "Are there any smells or anti-patterns appearing? Do we still follow our vision? Is everyone on board?"

I let my team know what I am doing during this time so the time is not taken from me. I think it is important to have time for visioning and not just time to work through tasks.

I ensure I get solid, unbroken chunks of time throughout the day (such as all afternoon each day, or two full days a week) without any meetings so that I can write code and pair program with other developers.

I give as much responsibility (always slightly more than you think you should) to other members of the team. This frees up my time, and the members often find it much more fulfilling to own whole parts of a system such as an integration point.

How do you strike the right balance between writing code and dealing with other issues?

Writing code is what I love doing most. However, quite often I deprioritise it in favour of resolving an issue that I notice would unblock more members of the team. I feel that people who understand both technical and business aspects are best placed to steer the team away from obstacles. They also tend to be better at finding solutions when the team does halt due to a block.

I try to avoid reviewing my team's check-ins. Instead, I ensure that the developers with more experience pair program on the critical stories. If I do not have a team member with that experience, then I spend much more time in the codebase.

I see myself as a guest in the codebase and not as the owner. I use the time in the codebase to detect code and architectural smells, anti-patterns, maintainability issues, and discuss these with the team. Ideally they will take ownership to resolve those. I also use the time to better understand the strengths of different developers, highlighting when they come up with a great idea and nudging them on how they might share that with a wider community.

Isabella's key question: How do I get opinionated developers with divergent opinions better integrated as a team?

I do not have a good answer to this. At the moment, I would say it takes time to build an understanding of why they do not like working with other people or consider other people's suggestions.

In the past I have sat with them and explained what I expected and why. I let them explain to me why they had a different approach. Normally there is some middle ground that can be found. But I would be interested to hear what other people do in these situations.

Isabella's background story

Isabella started working for ThoughtWorks in 2006 and began her Tech Lead journey in 2008. Since then, she has played the Tech Lead role for over eight different teams, mostly using Java and .Net Technologies. She has a Masters of Science in Electrical Engineering and Information Technology from the ETH Zurich.

It's Not About the Code – Patric Fornasier

What should a Tech Lead focus on and why?

Being able to master technology is absolutely necessary, but not sufficient in itself to deliver software effectively. Two other main areas that a successful Tech Lead should focus on are people and process. There is not much point writing great code, for example, if you are solving the wrong business problem, because you did not communicate enough with your customers. Or, it might make sense to have one developer work on something else other than stories, such as analysis, tech tasks, operations, or testing if this makes the team go faster. In this role, you make these cost/value decisions continuously and prioritise according to what you want the team to focus on.

As a Tech Lead, I spin many plates at once. What occupies my thoughts the most is figuring out which plates need to keep spinning and which ones I can afford to let crash.

Usually, my days are filled with making decisions

to strike a balance between cost and value in order to achieve an optimal outcome - short, medium, and long term. For example, I need to know my team well so that I can decide who is most suitable to work on a given task. There is a number of factors that influence this decision, such as task importance, task urgency, team-member skill set, experience, and personal preferences.

What has been your biggest challenge as a Tech Lead?

I think one of the hardest things is balancing short-term against long-term goals. It is easy to sell a short-term gain, but it requires more experience, discipline and skill to forgo a quick win today in favour of being in a better place tomorrow. One example that springs to mind, is when the Chief Technical Officer (CTO) of a large project I was working on asked me to add an extra day to our current iteration, because he had an important board meeting the following week and wanted to put us in a good light by demonstrating more progress than we had actually made. It was a tempting proposition in the short term but I knew it would backfire eventually.

It took some courage for me to stand my ground, but I explained that if he wanted to fake progress there are easier ways to do that. He abandoned his idea and presented actual data to the board, which went down well and avoided setting unrealistic expectations of what the team was capable of delivering.

Any time-management tips?

I try to get my priorities right. Generally, there's always more work than I could possibly do, so it is about deciding what's most important. I usually spend a few minutes in the morning writing down my priorities on a piece of paper, which I carry with me throughout the day. Every now and then, I take a couple of minutes to review the list or tick things off. Whenever I am spending more than a couple of minutes on something, I check the list to see if the task I am working on is actually the most important thing I should be working on. If it is not, I either stop immediately or take a minute to re-prioritise. That way, I am always fully aware that I am spending my time on what I decided was most important.

How do you strike the right balance between writing code and dealing with other issues?

Striking this balance is hard. Writing code takes long blocks of uninterrupted time and for a Tech Lead, these blocks become rarer. Even so, I think it is necessary that a Tech Lead spends time on the code base. A Tech Lead ensures the code base remains healthy. I don't think you can lead a team of developers if you do not know what you're talking about. As a principle, I don't ask a developer to do something that I would not do myself. It is a way to keep me honest and allows me to appreciate the work I ask others to do.

There are a few approaches to help me deal with distractions:

- Pair program - When I get distracted, my pair can continue working on the task. When I return, I find it easier to get back into the flow.
- Delegate work - I sit down with people when they're working on a crucial part. As soon as I feel they don't need me any more, I let them go on without me.
- Find quiet time - I try to take a couple of hours every week to either lock myself into a room or work from home until lunchtime.

Patric's key question: How do you keep your tech tools sharp?

I think there are really three essential parts to this: networking, alertness and learning. I am relying heavily on my professional network to filter and surface new ideas, tools, techniques, etc. At the same time, I pick up names or terms I am not familiar with. If I pick something up, I spend a moment putting it in context and understanding how it could be used. At this stage, my learning is superficial and I am only optimising for breadth, not depth, but it helps me build up a catalogue of resources that I can come back to at a later stage when I am confronted with a specific problem. At that stage, I spend more time to learn in depth. This, in combination with having a specific problem to solve, allows me to learn quickly and effectively.

Patric's background story

Patric has worked in commercial software for over 10 years, having spent time before that in academia. Although he enjoys coding, he finds himself always looking to improve teams and processes, which naturally led him into the Tech Lead role. He sees the most difficult challenge in software as the social rather than the technical aspects.

People Focus – Sarah Taraporewalla

What should a Tech Lead focus on and why?

I think about the following questions all the time:

- Is my team set up as well as it can be? And how do I get the best out of each team member?
- Does each team member know, understand and believe in the same goal?
- Am I allowing them enough room to make their own mistakes and grow, but not so much space that the project is derailed?
- Am I fostering a supportive environment where my team has the freedom to challenge me on my ideas?

What has been your biggest challenge as a Tech Lead?

I was on a team where the five developers doubled whilst I was away on holidays. Everyone had significantly different skills and experiences. I do not think I handled it as well as I would have liked, but I learned a lot.

One good thing I did was to identify the senior members of the team and delegated areas of functionality to them. They worked with me to come up with the high-level concept and design, but it was up to them to put it in code and explain it to the rest of the team.

As a result I worked closely with certain members of the team, and got to understand what was worrying them, where I should be concerned, where they wanted to extend themselves. But I did not spend enough time with the more junior members. I think they felt less appreciated and heard as a result.

Any time-management tips?

I use the story wall to let people know what I am working on.

I usually let highest priority (sometimes the "loudest shouting person") dictate what I am working on next and any other item purposely delay.

How do you strike the right balance between writing code and dealing with other issues?

That's hard! I find myself either refactoring code to enable stories in upcoming iterations, or sneaking a new, small story for myself. Depending on the size of the team, any contribution to code I make will not usually affect overall progress, so I don't fret when I am not working on stories. It frees me up to make sure I can pair with someone on tough stories, or stories which seem to drag. It also means that when I am dragged off to meetings the flow of a story isn't interrupted.

I set time aside specifically to sit down and pair, so on certain days no meetings may be booked.

I constantly have an ear open to discussions to work out if I am needed or not; that way I can carry on what I am doing, listen in and step in when I am most needed to cut down on time.

Sarah's key question: Was there ever a time when you thought that you weren't a good Tech Lead?

Yes, loads! Especially starting out. But I think that doubt makes you better at anything as you seek ways to improve. On my first large team as Tech Lead I had a crisis of faith that was so great I almost told our Resource Management not to make me Tech Lead, as I was certain I was doing something wrong, but couldn't figure out what. I consulted someone about it, who said, "You could avoid being Tech Lead or you could find out what you are doing wrong and fix it. What do your team mates think of you?" I didn't know the answer, so I started feedback sessions with everyone. It turned out that they thought I was doing a great job, but wanted me to spend a little more time with them. So we all learned together: they realised I was having doubts, so they helped me out and we became a much better team for it.

Sarah's background story

Sarah has been working in IT for about 10 years, starting with Boeing as a graduate and then moving on to ThoughtWorks three years later.

She stepped into the Tech Lead role as the second in command on a project for Ben Butler-Cole (BBC) and describes "unofficially falling into the Tech Lead role" again on her next project. Her subsequent Tech Lead roles have been in a fuller, more official capacity.

Engaging the Team – Glen Ford

What should a Tech Lead focus on and why?

As a Tech Lead, I aim to accomplish two main things:

- Remove the obstacles for my team: I address the issues that are holding back my team or individuals in the team, whether that be external issues such as blocking stakeholders, or internal ones such as lack of experience or knowledge.
- Make myself redundant: I work to ensure the team has the skills, knowledge, and experience to run itself. There are a couple of reasons for this: I want my teams to self-organise as much as possible; it gives them a greater feeling of empowerment. It means the team can operate without an over-

> seer, so I can have confidence, should I go on leave or get ill, that things will operate smoothly. Just as importantly, it also frees me up to look at broader concerns and add more value at a higher level.

My main worries as a Tech Lead are usually about people engagement. Technical problems are rarely insurmountable, in my experience. People problems are much more complex.

What has been your biggest challenge as a Tech Lead?

It is difficult to select the single most challenging situation. The most recent challenge was leading a strong team of four senior developers and technical architects, each with at least 10 years' experience and each had worked as Tech Leads in the past. All were very technically proficient and all opinionated.

The team had delivered a prototype very quickly, which had subsequently moved to production and, as a consequence, was falling apart at the seams with technical debt and design decisions that had made sense in the context of a prototype, but made no sense in production.

The challenge I had was getting the team engaged and working to a single vision; getting the best out of different personalities, whilst keeping everyone on the team talking and feeling part of the team.

If I hadn't been able to show my technical competence with this team it would have fallen apart, but because I had earned their respect, I was able to engage them on the surrounding issues we faced. I made it clear that my role was to remove their obstacles, manage the stakeholders, and clear a path to incrementally improve the system. In return I expected everyone to be professional, speak out when they felt things weren't right, and respect the ideas of shared ownership.

By treating everyone in the team as an individual and working to understand what they needed to perform to their optimum, I was able to make accommodations, which in turn built team camaraderie. For example, I fought hard to keep regular work-from-home rights for people who worked well remotely when these rights felt threatened by a management that tended to fall back on 'bums on seats'.

I worked hard building team interactions and I found productivity grew significantly. We built a team culture of 'disagreement is not criticism' and 'failure is learning where the boundaries are'.

Daily stand-ups were typically short; story cards were

simple cards, which were debated and rewritten until everyone understood. Process was at a minimum. I dealt with reporting to stakeholders and ensuring that no process without value crept into how we worked. Huddles (we sat together) several times a day became common, as we would solve specific issues as a group. We pair-programmed on occasion, but not as an explicit rule.

When I stepped into the leadership role the platform was causing operational pain and I had to stave off demands for rewrites, quick hacks, and other 'injected solutions'. I relied on my team's and my own technical competence in rebutting this, understanding that we needed to look unified and in agreement.

We turned the platform around from unstable, monolithic prototype to decomposed robust, distributed platform without any interruption to end users at all and we also delivered business value through new features and reduced costs.

Any time-management tips?

Starting early gives me an hour to get my thoughts and plans for the day in place. I'll go through anything outstanding from the previous day, review any urgent or important issues, of which I keep three to-do lists: one for today, one for near term and one for longer term. It just helps keep things visible to me.

I try and deal with issues face to face, rather than lengthy email exchanges. It is easy to burn a lot of time in email exchanges, which are open to misinterpretation.

How do you strike the right balance between writing code and dealing with other issues?

I tend to work on small discrete pieces of coding that are non-critical, so I don't hold up any team members. Or I work closely with another person, either pairing or close collaboration so that I can hand over seamlessly. This usually works well as I can address more Kaizen-type problems and reduce friction, which can otherwise build up, and it helps keep my knowledge of the codebase current.

I have occasionally coded deeply for work that represents major or complex functionality. However, on those occasions I did find it much harder to balance the needs of leadership against the 'mental space' required for such thought-intensive work.

Glen's key question: Have you received any training or mentoring specific to leading teams?

Many Tech Leads have had little to no training or guidance in what it means to be a Tech Lead, or how it requires a different mindset. On the contrary, I see many Tech Leads thinking that the role means having to do more hours than everyone else; that they have to be the best developer in the team.

I received minimal training in my engineering degree, but I have been fortunate to have worked with some great people in my career.

Glen's background story

Glen has worked in IT for 20 years after graduating with a degree in electronic engineering. He has lead about seven teams since 2000, moving between leadership and architectural roles.

The Tech of a Tech Lead

The role of Tech Lead would not be the same without the responsibility implied by the technical aspects of the role. At the same time, certain Tech Lead responsibilities distinguish the role from that of a developer.

Guiding the Technical Solution

The first distinguishing responsibility of a Tech Lead is their governance of a technical solution. This responsibility overlaps with a Technical Architect and in many organisations these two roles are one and the same.

The Tech Lead shapes the overall technical solution to ensure that *all* requirements are met. They need to appreciate all the functional requirements to understand what might be built as well as cross-functional requirements (CFRs) about how it might be delivered. The Tech Lead looks for the significant CFRs that could require a different architecture or additional work to improve dimensions, such as supportability or frequent deployability. The Tech Lead champions all relevant CFRs and educates people about the negative impact of neglecting them.

CFRs affect the shape of the final technical solution, so the Tech Lead uses diagrams to communicate understanding within the team.

Harmonising Team Direction

When you have a group of developers working on a single system, you will have occasions when developers disagree about how to approach a problem. Disagreements are healthy as long as the team settles on a direction relatively quickly. Disagreements become destructive when the team divides, unable to choose between alternatives.

Tech Leads watch carefully when the team reaches an impasse. They use different strategies to find ways for the team to move forward, perhaps facilitating, reaching for external advice, or sometimes stepping in to make a decision. In these situations, a Tech Lead first seeks agreement on the core problem being solved, before entertaining any solutions. Only once everyone agrees on the core problem will the team find a solution agreeable to all.

A Tech Lead also looks for signs that indicate developers may be moving in different directions. Tech Leads watch out for when an individual unnecessarily adds another way of solving a known problem. Different methods of accomplishing the same task leads to unnecessary complexity and makes collective code ownership more difficult. A team in harmony looks similar to a single developer writing the codebase, unlike the following:

A team out of harmony

A Tech Lead promotes design principles and architectural guidelines for developers to make decisions that align with the overall technical solution.

Managing Technical Risks

Technical risks quickly turn into issues that affect everyone who wants to change software, not just the developers. However, only people with a technical background can sense the risks and more accurately understand their impact. Developers are also be the first to feel the impact when risks become real and turn into issues.

The responsibility for managing and tracking technical risks falls to the Tech Lead. Just like the way a project manager tracks and resolves risks and issues, the Tech Lead works with developers to identify, prioritise and find ways to mitigate technical risks. The Tech Lead makes risks more visible to outside stakeholders and lobbies for time and resources to address them.

The Tech Lead finds different approaches to express technical risks to non-technical people. The Tech Lead uses metaphors and visualisations to explain to non-technical people the impact that taking risks might have. Expressing technical issues in ways non-technical people can understand creates better rapport and generates support for fixing them.

The champion for addressing technical risks or technical debt must come from within the team or the risks remain unaddressed.

Taking a Longer-Term View

A developer solves a problem based on their own experiences, knowledge, and what they think is right for them. A developer makes this choice with a narrow perspective. The Tech Lead has to approach problems with a wider perspective; they look at the consequences that a choice has on other people on the team, and the future work or rework that the choice could save or create. The Tech Lead evaluates decisions with a broader, longer-term view.

In the earlier section on Novices, new Tech Leads suddenly became aware for the first time of the impact a design decision could have on deployment, architecture, and the long-term maintainability of the system. What may be simple for a developer could make running the software in production more difficult and a Tech Lead needs to be aware of who might be affected by that choice, particularly if they sit outside of the team.

A Tech Lead becomes particularly concerned if a choice today makes it more difficult to change or add to the system tomorrow. The Tech Lead finds opportunities to safely expose a developer to this broader view to grow the developer's awareness of the impact an individual decision might have on the future.

Teams and Architecture – Simon Brown

What should a Tech Lead focus on and why?

The term Tech Lead is ambiguous: some consider the Tech Lead to be the lead programmer; some see it as a synonym of software architect. I prefer Software Architect, because it implies a set of responsibilities that aren't so obvious when you use the term Tech Lead.

Whatever term you use, the role should focus on putting together the high-level architecture of the software system, taking care to understand any requirements or constraints that influence the architecture. Architectures need to evolve over time and focus needs to be put on continuous technical leadership too, to guard the architecture and ensure technical quality.

To answer the question, I would have to say focus on making yourself replaceable. It is about coaching, collaborating with, and leading the team.

What has been your biggest challenge as a Tech Lead?

My biggest challenge was probably when I was asked to take over a software project because the previous Tech Lead quit. From the outside, the project appeared to have clean architecture, a great team who were on track to delivering within budget, and agreed time scales. On closer inspection it was a different story.

I felt that the architecture was overly complex. Future strategy was cited as the reason for this, but to date, this strategy has never been implemented! I fought to simplify the architecture, but too much had already been spent on those parts of the system that I felt were unnecessary. The code looked more complex than it should have too, and members of the development team complained about the complexity of the internal layering strategy. There were few automated tests; the development process being followed by the team was ambiguous, and the overall scope of the project was vague.

I had a choice: clean up the code, write tests and hope that everything worked itself out, or step back and revisit the basics, such as the scope of the project and the process that we should follow? I decided to do the latter, as no one had a clear idea of how much had been completed, or how much was left to do.

We set up some workshops with the project sponsors to define the high-level scope. We simplified the architecture; created a Kanban board to visualise the remaining work; introduced a simple definition of "done" and got serious about automated tests. We got there in the end, but it was the most frustrating project that I've ever been involved with.

It taught me two key things: a good team is more than the sum of its parts, and that not everybody has attention to detail. My first rule now for anybody in a leadership role is: never make any assumptions.

Any time-management tips?

There are lots of techniques for time management, including Getting Things Done and Personal Kanban. I think the key is to take a pragmatic stance of when something is "done". It is incredibly satisfying when you've written or re-factored some code to be the best it can be; the trick is to know when to stop. Automated tests and acceptance criteria do go some way to helping here, but "continuous re-factoring" does require some limits.

Things like documentation take a lot of time, so I work iteratively, pushing stuff out before it is done, to get feedback that I am heading in the right direction. That's the advice I would give anybody: we talk about building software using agile and iterative approaches, but these approaches can be useful in other aspects of a Tech Lead's day job.

How do you strike the right balance between writing code and dealing with other issues?

Firstly, don't take on more than you can handle. Secondly, don't put yourself on the critical path with regard to delivering code. It's not always possible, of course, but be aware that you can easily become the bottleneck. Thirdly, be open, coach, and collaborate. Sharing the Tech Lead role (even a little) spreads the pressure of other pesky issues that take away your time from writing code.

Stepping away from the keyboard can be uncomfortable when you first move into a leadership role, but you don't lose the ability to code by stepping back from your IDE (integrated development environment) for a few hours a day, so don't let it worry you.

Simon's key question: Where do you learn about technical leadership, and particularly the softer side of the role?

This topic isn't given much thought. There's a lot of discussion in the software industry about being agile and having self-organising teams, and the traditional view of software architecture has discouraged people from learning about the discipline. While I agree that we should certainly strive to be self-organising, most teams that I've seen are some way from that goal. Many problems they face can be solved by having a single, dedicated Tech Lead. I recommend these books:

- Becoming a Technical Leader by Gerald Weinberg
- Notes to a Software Team Leader by Roy Osherove
- Presentation Zen: Simple Ideas on Presentation Design and Delivery by Garr Reynolds
- Gamestorming: A Playbook for Innovators, Rulebreakers, and Changemakers by Dave Gray et al.

Simon's background story

Simon has spent 12 years working for IT consulting companies in a broad range of industries, gradually growing into the Tech Lead role. He moved back to Jersey in the Channel Islands just over four years ago.

Simon still writes code today but more of his work is helping teams understand software architecture, technical leadership and finding the balance with agility. He is currently writing a book, "Software Architecture for Developers" that covers these topics.

Enablement and Solution Design – Marten Gustafson

What should a Tech Lead focus on and why?

Enablement and solution design.

Enablement should come first and foremost. Ensure the team has room to work effectively; shield it from company politics, pointless meetings, and other distractions. At the same time, focus on transparency by describing what is happening around the team, changes in direction from the business or what may be coming up in the future.

Solution design comes a close second. I try to identify work patterns over time. I ask questions such as: "Do we write the same function more than once and, if so, can we consolidate the different versions?" or "Is our current data store a good fit for other data?" or "Should we use a different language for everything, or just for certain components?"

I track progress primarily by reading, or at least skimming all the newly written code and reading about new techniques or evaluating frameworks.

I spend significant time thinking about deferred issues that could come back to bite us. Issues such as whether we're using the right strategy for data versioning persistent data, or if operational aspects such as metric collection and log retention are good enough. I worry about having enough supporting infrastructure for the development team, such as build servers, or shortening build times and making deployments smoother. I consider whether we are spending enough time on quality aspects such as stability, availability, and scalability.

I try to foster a culture where developers see beyond the green unit tests and also observe operational aspects such as deployability, monitoring, metrics, and changing server topologies.

I use this as a list of principles for a novice Tech Lead:

- Read as much code as possible
- Set as few rules as possible
- Code wins arguments
- Be your own harshest critic
- There's always a better way, but what is the most feasible solution right now?
- Always address operational aspects early on.

I make sure we do something outside work once in a while and try to talk about something other than work.

What has been your biggest challenge as a Tech Lead?

Explaining to management the complexity of migrating a complete software stack, while switching hosting provider at the same time. I think I did fairly well by drawing a dependency tree. We have to do this in order to do that, and so on, all the way up to the root node named "DONE". This is a coarse and large variant of the Mikado Method.

Another challenge is dealing with bad technical investments. Techniques that look fine, start fine, and then come crumble shortly afterwards. You have to reassess, readjust, and find the best alternative route. The transition cost is easily forgotten, especially the grey area of motivation: does a forced change of a framework or practice de-motivate your team or does it energise them?

Shaping the overall team to work against common goals and honour agreed best practices can be very challenging. It is harder under pressure when people "dig in" with a focus on shipping. It is easy to slip on basic technical quality such as deployability, operability, and clean code.

Any time-management tips?

I don't trust myself with keeping tabs on how much I work. I write everything down as it is the only way to be sure. I update a spreadsheet on a daily and weekly (in aggregate) basis. I record short comments on particular events and notable accomplishments per week.

Secondly, time off can be a good thing, not just for you but for your team, as they get to work without you being around. After 14 years, I still struggle to take time off; I am definitely my own biggest obstacle to taking time off.

I try to defer planning as much as possible until something must be done, or the perceived need to plan has been obliterated by changed circumstances. Deferring as many items as possible frees up time for code reviews and actual programming.

How do you strike the right balance between writing code and dealing with other issues?

If you enjoy programming, you have to learn to accept that Tech Leads have a battle and there will be ups and downs. I prioritise non-programming tasks if I feel it enables the team to do their job better. I have learned to handle interruptions better, because the Tech Lead is a point of coordination. I am conscious of what I want and the prerequisites for making it happen.

Find your power animal. When I am stressed by too much multi-tasking, I sift through technical issues to find something small and relatively easy to do. I drop everything for a couple of hours and fix it. Shipping code that fixes something, however small, quickly puts me in a better mood.

> *Editor's note: A power animal is a shamanic concept: it is a spirit that empowers and protects a person from harm.*

Marten's key question: What principles and beliefs do you have around organising and planning software development?

I believe in self-organisation; within my team, obviously, but ideally in other parts of the organisation that work with development too. I'm a firm believer in relative estimation, but preferably not in terms of story points. I strive for an open discussion where the affected people, regardless of organisational affiliation, reach an agreement on the top three to five priorities.

People then self-organise to work through that list, breaking items down into smaller tasks if necessary. The team prototypes, tests, and releases as necessary. I prefer not to work with calendar deadlines or fixed-release windows.

I think the biggest challenge is finding the initial opportunity to prove this method of working is successful.

Marten's second key question: How do you work with those people or those parts of the organisation that don't understand programming?

My approach depends both on the type of organisation and what kind of mandate and autonomy I have. I invite other parts of the organisation to the planning and follow-up process. Involving them in the process demonstrates how pointless it is to estimate the number of hours or to set dates and it shows that time is better spent developing and finding out what requirements really need addressing.

Marten's background story

Marten is a Swedish software developer and has worked in backend, datastore and infrastructure verticals for the past 14 years. Previously, he played the Tech Lead role for one of Sweden's largest websites for a team of 12. He finds his current Tech Lead role for a smaller team requires much more hands-on work.

Manage Tech Debt – Mark Crossfield

What should a Tech Lead focus on and why?

Design! As a Tech Lead the most worrying aspect of development is technical debt, and the introduction of messy code and coupling, which potentially slows the team down. I review the team's design decisions; my input is to provide continuity and a different perspective. Ensuring the whole team is going in the same direction and has the same understanding of the code base requires knowledge of the historical context. An appreciation of the finer points of the craft helps, such as knowing the appropriate times to introduce generalisation and abstraction.

I would describe my principles as lean and responsible. I believe developers should own responsibility over the whole process: from capturing requirements through to delivery and assurance that a feature continues to work in production. I don't believe in separating out delivery disciplines; they are intrinsically entwined and people should contribute wherever they can. Every developer needs to consider the impact of each action or inaction they make. A Tech Lead must ensure that value is delivered and I find myself ensuring that a team delivering a change is also delivering value, rather than exploring its own interests.

What has been your biggest challenge as a Tech Lead?

I struggle to identify one challenge greater than the rest. I think my biggest challenge is collaborative design. With a large code base it is important for the team to consider the impact of the decisions that it makes, and that these decisions are not made in isolation. I have found that most people tend to put off design or leave it to someone else.

Not wanting to dictate design decisions, feeling optimistic and not having a huge amount of experience in technical leadership, I gave the team quite a lot of freedom and autonomy in this area. While this allowed the team to scale up quite quickly, we felt the knock-on effects as we were slowed by the fragile nature of many parts of the code. I have found external development coaches helpful, and I am slowly finding conceptual tools that can be used to help find better solutions such as Hexagonal Architecture[15] and Connascence[16] along with collaborative drawing and

---

[15] http://alistair.cockburn.us/Hexagonal+architecture

[16] http://en.wikipedia.org/wiki/Connascence_(computer_programming)

whiteboard sessions to ensure everyone is on the same page. Delegating some technical responsibility helps too, as it allows me to quickly communicate a design issue to one person and have them provide continuity within the sub team.

Any time-management tips?

Triage is an important tactic. In a large team it is important to use your time in the most efficient way. When someone needs to talk, I try to find a few things out before committing: what is it they wish to talk about? who else needs to be involved? Is the person blocked by waiting for me, and how long will it take? What I try to establish is what would be the impact if I delayed or were not even involved. If I am under pressure I ask people to approach me in a few minutes or a few hours. If I am prioritising something else, I try to keep the list of people who are waiting for me, to ensure that the conversation isn't forgotten about. I use TeuxDeux, but am considering a move to Trello. I have a terrible short-term memory when context-switching a lot, and find it much less stressful if I can rely on technology to remind me who I need to have conversations with. It is important to keep track of unresolved and impending issues, because too often they fall through the cracks - especially when delivery schedules are tight.

When I am not discussing a change, I try to ensure that what I spend my time on is aligned to a goal. The goal may be improving stability, reducing complexity, spreading knowledge, or improving visibility. It is easy to become absorbed by what you are doing and stray from providing value to the team. I am particularly prone to being fascinated by a problem, which is a luxury that a Tech Lead does not have; their availability is often required urgently, so deep dives should be the exception rather than the rule.

The best piece of time-management advice I was given by a mentor is to work out which issues will have the most impact, and so which would provide the most value by being resolved.

How do you strike the right balance between writing code and dealing with other issues?

I would not say I have found a balance yet! I would rather be writing more code than I do, and I think it would be easier to improve design by doing so, but my other responsibilities take up quite a lot of time.

That said, I think the most important thing a Tech Lead can do to balance their time is to pair with another team member to explore a problem and find a solution. By pairing, you can minimise the impact of ducking out as and when required.

The key is to try not to do too much; taking on

responsibilities inevitably takes you away from the code base when, realistically, you are probably among the most qualified to work on it.

Where possible delegate whatever non-coding tasks you can, but establish boundaries and supervision. I found situational leadership theory useful, and whenever I delegate I consider the person's will and ability. This helps decide how closely you need to supervise their work.

Mark's key question: "What key technical principals are essential knowledge for Tech Leads?"

I believe it is important to understand the difference between long-term and short-term decisions. For example, external communication protocols and data structures such as JSON, RESTful approaches, HTTP, or SOAP are more important in the long run than internal application choices such as language choice, TDD, or persistence framework.

I recommend Tech Leads understand layered architecture, the principles of hexagonal architecture, domain-driven design, and the ideas around Connascence as well as techniques around refactoring to remove it.

Mark's background story

Mark is the Technical Architect for Trader Media (Auto Trader) and has worked as a developer for eight years. He has worked as a Tech Lead for the last four years currently with a team of 16 developers on a long-term project.

His interests include system design, data visualisation, monitoring and resilience, and software quality, although he is particularly interested in code craftsmanship and the academic aspects of language and computing.

An Architect Too? - Tomi Vanek

What should a Tech Lead focus on and why?

There are two dimensions to the Tech Lead's responsibility: technology and people.

In terms of technology, Tech Leads face complex challenges that require intuition to recognise the root cause; they cannot be distracted by symptoms. The architect part of the Tech Lead specifies the shapes, patterns, inner structure, logic of the solution, and holds the map. The Tech Lead builds this map through design discussions with the team and then implements it with the team. The architecture should be specified just in time, so it has minimum fixed shapes. The Tech Lead ensures the architecture evolves throughout the lifetime of the system. I think of architecture as like a human body: it grows quickly at the beginning, in adult age it is kept in good shape, and knows when to give way to the next generation.

In terms of people: Tech Leads have to listen and observe the team to gather the critical mass of information to make the right decisions. They also need to understand the culture, historical background, and the people who developed and maintain the software system. A system needs to be adapted to the culture it lives in, particularly considering those who will continue to develop and maintain it. The Tech Lead must also adjust the development process to the team that builds the software. They must appreciate each person has their own dreams, sorrows, and unique personality. In a short space of time, the Tech Lead must find the right role for each person in the team and bring a harmonised rhythm to the team.

What has been your biggest challenge as a Tech Lead?

I coached an architecture team for a client. The team worked with a complex architecture, which paralysed development. It meant that the development team couldn't deliver new features or applications. The team knew the architecture was painful, but it was their baby; some felt its complexity demonstrated their technical expertise; for others, it represented job security.

I felt it was important to agree some basic values to roll out a new architecture. We settled on simplicity. We developed it together with the client's architecture team so they had some emotional investment in it and felt ownership for the new system.

A core feature of the old architecture had been locking to prevent concurrent editing of the same data. This was typical old-school, object-oriented programming. The feature required about 50 classes, deep inheritance chains, and was bloated with functionality, just in case.

I suggested to the team that we focus on features used by applications in production. The architects agreed and started to remove unused functionality, preserving only the two or three classes necessary. New services did not require any further explanation, as they were clear and simple.

Any time-management tips?

Managing time is hard; I am constantly looking for better ways to do it.

My simplest method is to work with a prioritised backlog of tasks of the same granularity. I then visualise the system on a board for the team and external stakeholders to demonstrate what I am working on. A visual sense of tasks completed, in progress, or waiting makes it easier for the team and stakeholders to see what I am working on.

I set aside some time in my day to read technology news on the internet. I find time to read on my commute to and from the office.

How do you strike the right balance between writing code and dealing with other issues?

I approach my Tech Lead tasks much as I always did as a developer. Looking at the development process is like finding an algorithm. Understanding communication problems between analysts writing functional specifications and developers is like debugging. However, when a Tech Lead moves away from coding, they cannot identify and fix certain issues.

I set time aside to write code. I also ask myself whether a particular task really requires my attention. I try to work on these together with other team members so the solution lasts beyond my own influence and the team evolves and refines the solution over time.

Tomi's key question: Where do you see yourself five years from now?

I really do not know ? that's the exciting thing about what we do!

Tomi's background story

Tomi has worked with software for more than 25 years and with a variety of teams for the past 15 years. He has worked in everything from software used in nuclear power plants to modern web applications and portals.

His current interest is developing a "just in time" approach to software architecture and using agile methods to program at a team level.

Champion Quality – Peter Moran

What should a Tech Lead focus on and why?

I focus most of my thoughts on two main concerns:

- How to develop good software design principles and practices in people;
- How to get the best out of technologists working together in teams.

When you have people who know their technology well and how to apply it sensibly, and they are motivated and can collaborate with those around them, you have the basis for high-performing software delivery. These are learned skills that can develop in the right environment with the right leadership; I believe a good Tech Leader needs to work hard to foster them and help individuals and teams grow in their capabilities in these areas.

What has been your biggest challenge as a Tech Lead?

For me, this was leading a team of 25 talented people to deliver a new, high-profile website under heavy time pressures. The technical challenges were keeping both quality and throughput high without sacrificing the good design principles that allow a system to be extended, maintained and to perform over a long period of time. Keeping technical debt low while under pressure is extremely hard. The people aspects were to keep talented technologists (developers, testers, ops administrators) motivated to stick to their principles and see the bigger goal, while features were stacking up and complexity grew. Balancing these sometimes competing objectives was extremely challenging. One key to handling the challenges (and not something I always do well) was communication. For example:

- Keep people informed
- Seek constant feedback
- Take time to discuss technical issues with as many team members as possible
- Minimise surprises
- Make sure everyone on the team understands the objectives of what you are trying to achieve
- Give everyone a voice; and
- Be prepared to fight for what the team tells you.

Any time-management tips?

I rely on keeping a small list of things to do and making sure I complete them each day. I also find it helps to keep my email inbox empty (I consider no unread emails as being empty). I've found that I needed to learn when to back out of things. It is ok to get involved in a range of technical issues, business discussions, or people management tasks, but I need to be aware of when to let go and trust others to take them to completion.

How do you strike the right balance between writing code and dealing with other issues?

I realise that I will not get to code as often as I want, but I put time aside to make sure I do. I will pick up small features or issues that are useful but not time-dependent and I spend a couple of hours each week getting them done. I try to pair at least once a week; I can get involved in a story knowing that if I am diverted there is someone else to run with it. This is a great way of keeping up with the codebase, and learning new practices and techniques. I also use code as therapy; whenever I have a window of opportunity, I'll code, because I'll feel better for it, and I am confident I can make the codebase better in some small way.

Peter's key question: How do you keep your technical people motivated?

Dan Pink, author of Drive has really good insights on this, and I've followed his approach closely. He doesn't cover one important aspect, though: the personal connections that make groups of people work effectively together.

Peter's background story

Peter is the Development Manager at Hooroo.com[17]. His role includes leading the delivery team in all aspects - technical, process, and people. He acted as the Tech Lead role on about 15 different teams and projects before that.

Peter is a software developer at heart and takes great care in sharpening his technical skills, as relevant skills help him more effectively lead teams. His interests continue in well-designed object-oriented software and developing skilled, motivated teams that deliver effectively.

---

[17] http://www.hooroo.com

Don't Forget Cross-Functional Requirements – Christy Allmon

What should a Tech Lead focus on and why?

My role as Tech Lead changes depending on the team size, its day-to-day activities, my own day-to-day activities, and what stage of the development cycle we are at. In general, I think my current role is SME for the Application (everyone – Analysts, Developers, Scrum Master, Testers, Integration Teams, and Customers – comes to me with questions and problems), as well as person who decides the priorities and technical/application direction to be taken.

The principles that concern me the most are: - Maintainability: the code has to be maintainable! I think some developers and contractors don't consider the fact that others have to come in after them and need to be able to maintain and troubleshoot the code. A lot of tools that are now available can help with measuring this, but having been on legacy systems as well as development efforts, my experience has been that an application is only as good as its maintainability.

- Hard coding: do everything you can to avoid hard coding. If there is any way at all to avoid hard coding a value that, in my experience, will change, do it! If it is client-based (I work on Java Swing fat client), put it in a property or other kind of file. If it is server-based (backend of the application), put it in a database or provide some kind of client-triggered event. Even if you think it will never change, it inevitably will.
- Performance: I often have to make suggestions and verify that performance has been considered in the logic of the code. For example, if you are loading or processing data multiple times, be mindful of doing the static stuff only once. Also consider on-demand or just-in-time processing where applicable.
- Stability: weighing up the risk of a particular change against the impact it may have on stability. My contractor developers often have good suggestions for bringing in new approaches or tools, but I have to weigh up the benefits against the risks.

What has been your biggest challenge as a Tech Lead?

I would have to say that the situation I am currently in is my most challenging yet. My typical day involves so many meetings or team discussions that I am in a constant flux of having to context switch and I find it difficult to complete any particular task. On top of that, it is rare that I get a chance to code, which is the part of my job that I really enjoy and honestly what I am really good at. I am trying to do more and more teaching as things as they come up so that my team can be more self-sufficient and help each other instead of relying on me. I am working on delegating more so that I have time for the important things and to get me back to a state where I can contribute with doing some of the coding. In the past, I often did much of what I like to call "heavy lifting" coding: the complex or critical pieces of the application that required my expertise and skills. I haven't been able to do that for quite a few months due to the environment we are currently in, but I hope to get back to that soon.

Any time-management tips?

I have to prioritise in order to manage the demands on my time; I have to say no to some things or delegate what I can. I also know that there are times in a release cycle that will require overtime. It is cyclical and part of the job and if you understand that it will all eventually come out in the wash; you can manage it. My family has come to learn this important concept and knows that there will be times when I have to work a bit more than others. But again, to counteract these busy times, there are also lulls. During these lulls I can re-energise myself and catch-up on some of the less critical things in preparation for the next busy cycle. Learning this and understanding it has helped me to deal with it over the years. I have had to mentor many young professionals on this very subject so they can learn how to deal with the stresses and time management during the upswings. It is rewarding to see them get through the high-effort times and see them relax during the lulls to get ready for the next big push.

How do you strike the right balance between writing code and dealing with other issues?

As I mentioned above, my current role has resulted in limited code writing and it is been difficult to deal with personally. I am working on doing all I can to get back to it though. Part of this struggle has been bringing my team to a place where they have more knowledge about the application and more confidence in their own decision-making abilities. It has to be a trade-off that I drive through and part of it is me letting go of some of that control to them

– my confidence in them to do what's expected. In that respect, I am trying to take opportunities to teach as well as to delegate. It is a long process and one that won't immediately result in me getting back to writing code – but hopefully in the long run, it will benefit me as well as the team.

Christy's key question: What do you think are your greatest contributions to the team as a Tech Lead?

My greatest contributions to this team are my application expertise (I just know where all the bones are buried) and my general development and problem resolution know-how!

I have been asked to provide a teaching session to my team on how I go about resolving issues and specifically geared towards a couple of issues that came up recently. I would like to think that some of my expertise on this subject is knowing how to go about getting to the bottom of an issue and not tied specifically to this application. As I mentioned before, I am really good at this part of the job – whether it is learned or natural – probably a little bit of both. One of the reasons I was asked to do this was that it took me 30 minutes to solve an issue that numerous members of the team had worked on for two whole days without resolving. How was it that I could find and fix the issue in such a short amount of time? Especially not having been in the code for a long while? I put together a general document outlining my thought process and the questions I ask myself when faced with an issue like the one we had and then shared that with the team.

The application expertise just comes with time in the code and taking the time and effort to apply it to memory. However, I also suspect that many developers don't bother to get to the crux of a problem, functional area, or application and simply gloss over the surface, focusing on "what" it is. I think the fact that I often want to know the root cause of why a problem has occurred has helped me become a Tech Lead, as I am more able to answer the difficult questions of whether we can do something or what is likely to happen if we do it. If you don't look at "why" as well as "what", you cannot really get to that level of understanding. This same approach is also applicable to the problem-solving I mentioned before and part of what I shared.

Christy's background story

Christy's skills in analysis, code, and resolving problems made her a perfect fit for the Tech Lead role, which she has played with Fortune 500 companies for the past 27 years.

Prioritising Tech Tasks – Chris Close

What should a Tech Lead focus on and why?

The most important thing to consider in a Tech Lead role is when it makes the most business and technical sense to perform architectural modifications/refactoring. If these important tasks aren't done at the right time, the solution will spiral into a mess. But if you do too much of it, the business might not "see" any actual benefits.

What has been your biggest challenge as a Tech Lead?

I had a tough time attempting to schedule in tech tasks into a sprint with the business. After trying to resolve the situation myself with the product owner, I had to get managers higher up to agree that the work was beneficial to the end product and then had the work scheduled in over several sprints/iterations.

Any time-management tips?

Ensure you have a good team of people that you can hand over work tasks to. This means that you can feel confident in using your time for high-priority tasks/issues relating to investigations or analysis. Of course, you still need to check in with the team on how these tasks are progressing and provide assistance where necessary, but it doesn't require large, continuous blocks of time.

Another good idea is to keep all work in progress visible to you and the team. This way anything important will be talked about in daily stand-up meetings. You are then also in a better position to leverage their time later on as they are aware of the progress on these tasks.

How do you strike the right balance between writing code and dealing with other issues?

This can be difficult due to interruptions to address issues that crop up. This can be solved by pairing for code-writing, so that you can deal with issues or short conversations for a few minutes and return to the code while still maintaining momentum in the coding task at hand.

You need to have a balance and still keep your hands in the code so that you can make good decisions later on based on the infrastructure of the code that has been created.

Chris's key question: How do you feel confident that the work scheduled is ready to be done by developers in your team?

While it may not make sense in terms of efficiency to undertake a large amount of up-front technical analysis before a story is started (because a story may never be started), it is important that a task can be fully understood by any developer that is about to start work on it.

There are a couple of strategies to achieve this:

- Ensure the team is aware of the breadth and depth of a task while it is being planned. Any assumptions for the stories should be included in the detail of the story, but can be flexible, based on technical common sense and business needs - all parties being in agreement, of course.
- When a task is started, hold a whiteboard session where the team brainstorms different ideas and solutions so that everyone knows how to move forward with the work.

Chris's background story

Chris has been working in software development for 12 years and first acted as a Tech Lead in 2007. He moved into his current Tech Lead role in the past year and most of his work is with .Net web technologies such as MVC4.

Bridging the Business with Tech

When a developer becomes a Tech Lead, their relationship with other parts of the business becomes stronger. The responses in this section outline why those relationships are important and describe how the nature of the relationship changes.

Building Trust

As a Tech Lead, you spend more time with non-technical stakeholders and this is a good opportunity to build trust. Non-technical stakeholders are suspicious of where time goes, because software involves so much that is intangible. The Tech Lead must constantly manage the perception that too much time is being spent on activities that may not have any obvious visible return on investment. I have found that companies with roots in a more traditional retail background are more susceptible to this perception.

The Tech of a Tech Lead highlights the need to spend time working on technical tasks and how gaining the trust of non-technical people gives the development team more freedom to do what they think necessary. One of the best ways of building trust is best summarised by the following quote[18]:

> From a trust perspective, continuous delivery is the ultimate in frequent, trust-building gestures.
>
> — Jason Yip (@jchyip)

Nurturing trust with non-technical stakeholders takes time. Tech Leads find a way to balance time between the team and those that sit outside the team. Finding this balance is a struggle; some of those interviewed discussed how easy it was to end up in *too much* technical detail.

Finding Time for Technology

A Tech Lead manages technical risk and champions the need for time invested in quality, but this can only be done with trust from other parties. Finding enough time is a constant challenge. When the team spends too much time on software quality without delivering value, you risk breaking the trust you have built.

---

[18] https://twitter.com/jchyip/status/371823213421928448

Fortunately, spending time on quality issues has a direct positive impact on end-users or the business, by making the user experience better and faster, for example, or resulting in fewer requests for help and assistance.

Spending too little time on software quality leads to internal quality issues and quickly turns into visible external quality issues. Managing the Technical Debt[19] is a key skill for the Tech Lead.

Every developer has their own perception of acceptable quality. Some want to perfect their code, spending significantly more time over it; others take a hack-and-slash approach that favours fast feedback but results in an unmanageable mess. The Tech Lead is ultimately accountable and must monitor where and when to take each approach based on value being delivered.

Making Technology Solutions Easy to Understand

Developers are stereotyped as having poor communication skills. You probably recognise the characteristics: - they go on endlessly about technical detail, not pausing to ask questions of the other person or even

---

[19] http://martinfowler.com/bliki/TechnicalDebt.html

ensuring they are on the same page; they assume that the other parties know all the terms they are using and the broader context.

A Tech Lead has to develop the essential skill of helping non-technical people understand and relate to the technical issues when necessary. They draw upon the communication tools of simple diagrams, collaborative whiteboard sessions, metaphors and simple, clear language with minimal (or better yet, non-existent) use of acronyms and technical terms. They put themselves into the shoes of non-technical people and anticipate when a technical detail might be important, introducing technical terminology in a non-threatening manner that does not leave the other person feeling stupid. They educate with care because they recognise that some people do not want, or need, to know a certain level of technical detail.

The Tech Lead is constantly aware that not all problems can, or should be solved by technical solutions. The Tech Lead builds trust with non-technical people. Only after gaining trust can a Tech Lead describe the downfalls of a particular solution more openly, describing why one technical solution proposed may fail to solve the problem. They also work to pass on the necessary communication skills to other members of the technical team so the business does not rely on a single person. They provide feedback to developers when they witness a non-technical person being overwhelmed by technical jargon and encourage the use of whiteboards to visualise and find differences in understanding between technical and non-technical members.

Influencing Planning

Organisations look to the Tech Lead for input during budgeting and planning cycles. Zero involvement from the team often leads to over-commitment and technical risks being overlooked. A strong relationship built on trust creates opportunity for the Tech Lead to influence the planning process.

During this planning process, the Tech Lead spots business opportunities to use technology based on low effort, or to bring visibility to high areas of technical risk. The Tech Lead is careful not to over-commit, as they are aware they do not know everything; committing the team without its involvement creates future tension if the plan goes wrong.

> Under promise and over deliver - Tom Peters, from "In Search of Excellence"

The Tech Lead's influence over the planning process is potentially great, but you must beware of spending too much time on it. Involvement in planning processes eats into time a Tech Lead spends with the team and the codebase. The more time a Tech Lead spends away from the team and the code, the more likely they too will underestimate complexity or unknowingly take on additional risk.

Involvement in the planning process gives the Tech Lead greater insight into upcoming areas. Knowledge about plans for the future makes for better decision-making, particularly when arbitrating between what-if scenarios in the codebase.

Championing Business Needs

As you spend more time closer to the business, the Tech Lead appreciates what is truly important to the business. The Tech Lead uses this knowledge to make the team more aware of their operating context. The Tech Lead clarifies the current goal and reminds the team how their software moves the business towards the goal.

A clearer understanding of the real goal helps developers make better choices. For example, one design may require more manual processing by end-users, but the software function may cater for an edge case and the return on the time invested by the development team may not be high enough and could make changing business processes difficult in the future.

In contrast, if an error in the software threatens essential cashflow for the business, regardless of how rare, the development team might spend additional time building a quality design.

Technical choices rarely exist outside of a business context where time is constantly traded off with the hopes of better returns. The Tech Lead builds awareness in the team that goes beyond the keyboard and the systems being built.

The Big Picture – Luca Grulla

What should a Tech Lead focus on and why?

A Tech Lead has to clearly grasp the big picture of the project. They need to understand what the expected business goal is and help a team to transform that idea into a system.

To achieve the goal they have to find the delicate balance between a delivery pace that satisfies business needs and maintain an overall technical quality that enables long-term returns.

What has been your biggest challenge as a Tech Lead?

I find the biggest challenge is in co-ordinating and mediating business needs with technical needs.

A few years ago, I joined a project struggling to meet a fixed deadline. The deadline was strict due to the specific nature of the business and missing it would have significantly affected the project's return on investment.

I saw problems at different levels:

- A product owner that often changed their mind
- A team constantly interrupted and sidetracked with extra features
- A team struggling with motivation to meet the deadline

In this context, I focused on several areas:

- Shaking up the team to clarify the serious implications of the deadline and ensure we put in extra effort.
- Working with developers to identify the parts of the system causing the most pain, and planning how to improve or rewrite them whilst delivering the planned features.
- Monitoring the extra features to avoid unnecessary scope, and working closely with the business owner to identify those features that added business value and were essential to deadline.

Any time-management tips?

Although Tech Lead time is precious, it is important to be available to anyone who needs to talk. I try to create an environment where people know I am there to help, both from a business and from a technical perspective. I encourage people to come and talk freely to me. If I cannot respond immediately, I try to get back to them as soon as possible.

I try to minimise time in formal meetings. Although I am sent many meeting invitations, I never decline them. If I do not feel I would add much value to the meeting, I ask the organiser about the goal of the meeting and their expectations of me. If they confirm my suspicion, or I am not interested in the content, then I ask if it is okay to skip it.

Instead of formal meetings, I prefer an environment where others feel comfortable talking to me casually. Handling decisions in a less formal way is often more time effective. Obviously, this is not always possible because people in different roles have different expectations, in which case I try to plan ahead so that I don't have to keep jumping into things.

How do you strike the right balance between writing code and dealing with other issues?

It depends on the needs of the project; a Tech Lead needs to be slightly less hands-on sometimes. Tech Leads need to develop a "sixth sense" skill of understanding what is high priority given the context. Sometimes you feel the project needs more support from a business perspective; sometimes you have to appreciate that the team is wrestling with technical issues where you can help by being directly involved. The tricky part is not letting one of the two aspects take 100 per cent of your time for too long. I have found it is particularly easy to become heavily involved in the business side of the problems for a certain amount of time to lose track of the technology.

There are periods where I'm aware I can't contribute much to the overall technical delivery and I try to stay in the loop and focus on helping the team concentrate on our overall architecture. When my focus as Tech Lead is giving input to the business side, such as advice and technical support, I keep browsing the codebase to understand the overall direction. I talk with the rest of the team about the daily problems they are trying to solve. Informal chats to and from lunch are great for this. I keep a close eye on the story flow on the wall to have a mental map of how the system is growing. If I feel we are losing direction, I try to remind the team of the overall plan and what the expected business value is. I might do this following the stand-up, or with an impromptu gathering with all the technical people at the end of the day. If another team member is strongly advocating a change of direction, I might sit with them to understand their reasoning and to find out if they have discovered a better direction than the one currently planned.

I try to set aside dedicated time so that I can code without interruptions. An ideal, for me, is half a day. Sometimes I book time out. If I'm approached with a non-urgent issue while I am coding, I offer to address it later in the day. People are okay with, "Can we talk about this later?" as long as I offer an alternative time get back to them. Make sure you actually do get back to them when you agreed and don't postpone again at the last minute as you will start to lose trust with your team. This approach gives me the ability to focus on coding when I start pairing, but still makes me available for others' needs.

Luca's key question: What is the most urgent lesson a Tech Lead should learn?

As Tech Lead, you will be pulled in many different directions. You will be occupied with the overall architecture; providing input to and supporting the business; discussing and planning for the path to production, and sometimes reshaping the team by rolling people in (or out). With so many different responsibilities, you need to accept that you will not be able to influence every part of the system. In this role, you can have the final word, but use it wisely. If you see something you do not agree with, ask yourself, "Is it jeopardising the overall success of the project? Or is just a matter of my personal taste?"

Your role should be to keep on top of technical issues that might lead to a project failing. You must learn to recognise and accept feasible alternative solutions - not just your own, and particularly if it is not what you might do if in the same position. Working with the team to develop alternative solutions engages them and creates a strong sense of ownership. Doing it all yourself introduces the risk of you becoming the bottleneck and a single point of failure.

Luca's background story

Luca has lead about six teams in his 12 years working with technology. His current role is acting as a Senior Software Engineer at uSwitch[20]. Before that Luca spent four years at ThoughtWorks as a Tech Lead.

---

[20]http://uswitch.com

Align Technology with Business – Robert Annett

What should a Tech Lead focus on and why?

The Tech Lead keeps the team on track to deliver the *business* requirements, while making sure these are within the non-functional requirements.

It is easy for a development team to lose sight of what their employer actually wants and instead focus on their own goals. For example, they worry more about using cool technologies or hitting an arbitrary unit test coverage metric rather than what the end user actually needs.

What has been your biggest challenge as a Tech Lead?

My most challenging situation was one where the main end user wanted the project to fail. This is more common than most IT workers realise; most people don't like change and a replacement IT system may endanger the current user's job. This often leads to users deliberately withholding information and opposing reasonable functionality.

How did I handle it? I admit: badly. Developers tend to look for technical solutions and for every "hand grenade" thrown by the end user, I tried to work around it as a technical problem. This leads to hard work and constant change. Ultimately it is a political issue and the solution is also political; for example, I could have tried to get buy-in from management to implement the change and stop any sabotage.

Any time-management tips?

Plan and keep an eye on the big picture. It is easy to get bogged down in the minutiae of a technical issue. You need to know when to 'declare victory' over a problem and move on.

How do you strike the right balance between writing code and dealing with other issues?

If you have responsibilities beyond writing code, they take priority and you need to ensure your code-writing tasks are not on the current critical path. This is to avoid blocking others' progress if you cannot work on it for a while. You also need to make sure you aren't the only person who knows a particular business area or technology for the same reason. Pairing with junior members of the team (on whatever they happen to be working) is good, as is pairing with anyone on the critical path.

Robert's key question: "How do you deal with conflicts within the team?"

These can be difficult for someone from a technical background. The key is to remain professional and not become emotional. Avoid sending email while you are annoyed. Be direct and honest. Stay calm, detached and mediate, but once you've listened to everyone then you must make a decision and stick to it. It is also good to let everyone have a victory once in a while. For example, if someone really wants to use a certain template for the wiki, let them.

Robert's background story

Robert has worked in IT since 1995. Most of his work has been with backend systems with large sets of data before the term "big data" became trendy. In that time he has played various roles, including a Tech Lead for a number of teams. His most recent experience was working in a "front office" role for a financial institute where he finds the role more reactive.

Mapping the Future – Jason Dennis

What should a Tech Lead focus on and why?

I worry about the technology being used and what we should be using for the future: is there a better way to do what we need to do? I also worry whether the code being produced by the team follows my design and coding guidelines; I am a bit pedantic about that sometimes.

I focus on improving performance; I want it quicker; I want Google speed, because customers won't wait for the page to load. I also want to focus on improving the team skills and developing skills that get people moving through the code issues faster so we can focus on bigger issues.

What has been your biggest challenge as a Tech Lead?

The most recent was a platform upgrade where we used an outside vendor for the project, but they didn't understand our business model and so made assumptions we could never support. One instance was the co-mingling of the admin and front-facing website into one site: I had to split them because mixing the admin with the website would bring all kinds of problems, not least of which were poor design choices by the vendor.

Even though time was extremely tight and people said it couldn't or shouldn't be done, I decided to do it because it was best for the company. I also designed the entire solution so it fitted best practices.

Any time-management tips?

I try to answer emails as they come so people don't send more emails asking why I haven't answered them. I also try and carve out set periods of time to focus on a task if I need to, but I try to avoid doing this if possible.

For projects I try my best to estimate correctly based on the assumption that I won't be working on the project all the time but will have other things to deal with.

How do you strike the right balance between writing code and dealing with other issues?

Balance is tricky and sometimes you just have to go with the flow of what is happening at the time rather than what you would like to be doing.

Jason's key question: How do I become a leader?

Learn and grow. You need to learn all you can, never sit still because you have enough to do in the job; keep on sucking down knowledge about new technologies and new best practices. Help others to grow in their role so you shine as a leader.

Jason's background story

Jason has been doing this since 1995 and has been around computers since 1982. He has played the Tech Lead role a few times at different organisations with both local and remote teams over the course of about nine years. His interests are varied, but when work allows he likes to work on remodelling his house as well as reading and keeping up with different technologies and seeing what is out there in the realms of technology.

Finding Balance with the Business – Cory Foy

What should a Tech Lead focus on and why?

I think the most important thing a Tech Lead should focus on is the balance between delivering customer value rapidly, and meeting the needs of the architectural plan. Too often, customers are asking us for things they don't know they don't know. They won't be able to give us meaningful feedback until we have delivered something, so the longer we wait before getting that feedback, the more wrong we could be. But that has to be balanced with a vision of the architecture to build a high-quality system. The trick is to deliver that vision by building small slices of value that are potentially shippable.

What has been your biggest challenge as a Tech Lead?

People and communication; I think for any Tech Lead, the people challenges trump just about every single technology one. When I worked at Microsoft, we were dropped into client sites where the systems were down and companies were losing lots of money. The way they trained us for that was by putting us through a three-week, soft-skills boot camp. For that reason, I recommend Tech Leads looking at the soft skills side, and books like Crucial Conversations: Tools for Talking When Stakes Are High, How to Argue & Win Every Time: At Home, At Work, In Court, Everywhere, Everyday and Behind Closed Doors: Secrets of Great Management.

Any time-management tips?

Make everything visible: for personal use, things like Personal Kanban are invaluable techniques. Visualising the work you have to do, and how long it is taking is invaluable.

I also don't worry about replying to every email immediately. I don't do Inbox Zero[21], but I do leave emails that need to be handled as unread. I then go back when I have free moments and sort by unread, and start working from the bottom up. It takes time, but I get to them all eventually!

How do you strike the right balance between writing code and dealing with other issues?

As a Tech Lead, my first responsibility is my team, not my code. That means I might work longer hours than other members to keep up with the "same" workload.

---

[21] http://inboxzero.com

Or I might not be able to take on as much work as them. Most of my time is focused on teaching and understanding the challenges of the team to ensure they are working as smoothly as possible. It is not always easy - there are certainly times when I just want to put on headphones and code, and so I do. But that cannot be all the time.

Cory's key question: How do Tech Leads prepare others to be Tech Leads?

I often see Tech Leads or architects who do not want to give their position up to others. We focus on mentorship and growth. The way that I prepare others is by pushing decisions to them and letting them make mistakes.

Cory's second question: How do you learn, grow and keep up with new technology?

I think one of the big ideas behind the craftsmanship movement is that you as an individual are responsible for your growth - not your employer, not your leads or your managers. I find it is important to take time to invest in yourself. Do some reading. Attend or present at conferences. Participate in user groups. All of these activities help prevent you becoming stagnant.

Cory's background story

Cory is a technologist and change agent. He loves software development and is passionate about growing organisations. He has worked with software for the past 15 years, working and speaking with teams all over the globe.

A Bridge to the Business – Ryan Kinderman

What should a Tech Lead focus on and why?

I have often told by project managers and other developers that I was the "acting" Tech Lead, which to me implied that I was the team member most effective in working with people to unblock the team, guide us to correct decisions on topics of software design, and help with areas such as project planning and expectation setting. That's what a Tech Lead has to do. It's possible to share lead responsibilities, or for a lead to relinquish or spread leadership responsibilities to focus on technical details for a while.

Technical projects are complex, and the principal thing that I feel I must do as a Tech Lead is act as the communication bridge between the non-technical and technical stakeholders on the project. As Tech Lead, I need to be able to explain technical concepts to non-technical stakeholders in a way that they understand and feel comfortable with. I must also justify the technical decisions being made to both non-technical and technical stakeholders, often comparing those decisions with possibly many available alternatives. I must also help the technical team understand the context for the functionality being built according to what I've learned by communicating with the project manager and/or client stakeholders. To be able to do this requires a wide variety of skills, both technical and interpersonal.

On the technical side of the project, other responsibilities include working with other technical team members to:

- Decide what technology to use
- Understand how to use the technology properly to deliver the desired functionality
- Establish an approach for the development that will be done to build the necessary features, including:
- How the development tasks should be broken up, organised, and prioritised
- Maintaining a high level of quality for what is developed
- Protecting developed functionality against regression as behaviour changes over time
- Earn the respect and trust of, and act as an equal to, the development team by participating

in code reviews and/or pairing on development tasks and facilitate an open discourse on decisions being made.

Given the breadth of skills and understanding required to be Tech Lead, it took me a while to narrow down the core responsibilities. Most of the time it isn't enough to cover only those core responsibilities. Sometimes a project lacks a project manager, or the project manager lacks the experience or knowledge to apply the right management process. Sometimes the technical team doesn't have the right skill mix, or there is a disproportionate number of junior to senior developers on the team. In such situations, the Tech Lead, if the project is lucky enough to have one, must assume some of the responsibilities of these other roles in order for the project to be successful.

What are your secrets to managing time?

When it comes to my work and professional life, I prioritise obsessively. I try very hard to make sure that I have a list of all of the things that need to, or potentially should eventually, get done across projects, goals, and contexts. I review this list regularly and make sure it's accurately prioritised. I then work through the items on the list one by one with a strong focus. I try and pause at regular intervals to check email or collaborate in other ways, sometimes as a result of items in my list, but usually to deal with external actors that are changing conditions outside of my focus that I need to stay abreast of and work into my own prioritised list.

By making sure that I have a prioritised list of things that I need to do, I generally know that I'm spending my time on the right things, in the right order. If it feels as though I'm not going to be able to accomplish time-sensitive items from the list, I raise this as a concern to others, and try to delegate or update people's expectations of when it will get done.

How do you strike the balance between writing code and dealing with other issues?

As Tech Lead, I often write code to gain an accurate understanding of the experience of a developer on the team I'm leading, and to communicate with the developers at an equal level. By coding with the developers on the team, or reviewing and providing feedback on their code, I learn about their personalities and development styles, as well as strengths and weaknesses, and they learn about mine. It is time-consuming though, and I don't have always have that luxury, especially in situations where I'm joining a project that has been underway for a while.

I need to have a broad, intimate understanding of the technologies being used, and a vision of the structure of the entities in the system and interactions between them. It usually turns out better if I spend time alone getting the application running on my development machine, tracing through the relevant areas of code, thinking about design implications, diagramming out nontrivial bits, writing test cases to confirm assumptions or answer questions on how things are working, and so on. I don't consult anyone during this process; I learn things on my own terms and come to my own understanding. Only after this process, do I check my assumptions and understanding with others. By following this practice, I learn things at a much deeper level, avoid bothering the team with tedious questions, and gain respect.

In addition to pairing, development, and analysis of the system, I try and review every bit of code that goes into the system. It's often impossible to review and provide feedback on every commit, but at least by reviewing every commit, I can provide deferred feedback in various ways. If I notice software design issues emerging, I can consider including time to address them when scoping future work.

Some activities - product review meetings, high-level scoping, breaking development tasks out for upcoming cycles - take time from reviewing or working with the code going into the system. Some things I need to participate in, but relatively infrequently, usually once a quarter or so. I think it's important to try and time this hands-on work to be done during stable or inactive periods for the project. Product review meetings can usually be attended by a development or project manager, who will report back to me and the team. Breaking development tasks out for upcoming cycles can generally be distributed to the development team as development tasks themselves. This approach may not work if the team is primarily junior or has issues, but the project should be restricted in such cases anyways. Regardless, I will try to take on any or participate in particularly tricky or critical development break-out work myself.

Sometimes, if there are greater issues that detract from my time to review or write code, I assess whether the team can maintain a reasonable level of code quality for a period of time, while I address those issues. If there is someone on the team that I can lean on to keep the bar for quality high, I might do that. If I don't feel able to leave the team to maintain code quality, I let the project manager or client stakeholder aware of this fact, and the cost of continuing development. By doing this, I afford them the opportunity to set proper expectations, budgets, or whatever is necessary to correct the situation, or deal with the potential consequences I've identified.

Ryan's key question: What activities are important for a Tech Lead to engage in outside of work to stay vital and relevant in the field?

Listed in order of importance:

1. *Maintain balance between work and life* I believe all developers including Tech Leads should spend time learning and improving their skills. Sometimes learning a new language or paradigm absorbs long periods of time that upset other parts of your life. I try to keep a healthy balance between professional growth and pursuing my other interests by breaking bigger tasks into smaller tasks that *can* be completed in a few hours.
2. *Develop a deep understanding of good software design, good practices and different development styles* Our industry is broad and deep with many specialities to learn from. I seek to learn about concepts that transcend any specific implementation or programming language. For example, the famous book Design Patterns became my bible because you can apply these concepts in many contexts and programming language, not just one specific platform, tool or product.

3. *Stay connected as much as possible on hard technical skills* Even though I will never know everything, it's useful to read and sometimes experiment with a wide variety of technologies. Reading in varied areas often ends up serendipitously relevant to a problem I am working on a week or two later. I try to read broadly across a wide variety of technologies and problem domains, such as writing a Linux kernel module through to the structure of an EPUB file. I pay for a subscription to a few professional publications such as "Linux Magazine" and "Communications of the ACM" on top of the websites and blogs I subscribe to. I experiment with projects on a small Virtual Machine (VM) lab at home built with Linux and kvm. Using VMs allows me to start and stop experiments quickly.

Ryan's background story

Ryan was interested in computers from around the age of 10 and knew he wanted to do something with computers when he grew up. He studied Computer Science at the University of Wisconsin, Oshkosh and after graduating went on to work for a US Bank as a software developer, where he learned as much as he could about user cases, agile methodologies.

He then moved to ThoughtWorks, where he learned about agile project management and development practices.

He has been a Tech Lead for about five years.

You

When I first read the responses in this section, each person seemed to focus on how *they* approached the Tech Lead role. One person described their approach changing as the context changed. Many Tech Leads also remarked on becoming more self-aware; especially remaining vigilant against being a bottleneck of information or decision-making ability in the team. What I especially enjoyed discovering from these interviews was an appreciation of how *you* can shape the Tech Lead role to best fit your skills and still be successful.

Adapting to New Circumstances

When a developer encounters a new problem, or a new library or programming language, they must draw upon new skills. Likewise, the Tech Lead must draw upon different skills to handle different situations. The skills required to be a part of a business planning cycle, for example, are significantly different from those required to manage technical debt.

Changes in the team also require a change in focus from the Tech Lead. A developer leaving the team may leave a knowledge gap or additional responsibilities. The Tech Lead monitors for gaps and finds ways to bridge them. In contrast, a new developer joining the team may have a completely different coding or working style and the Tech Lead must now find ways to realign the team integrating the approaches brought by the new person.

A Tech Lead has to handle many more varied situations than they did as a developer, often with little practice in new skills. You need to develop a broader skill set to better cope with these new situations. Attend training courses or read books that improve your communication skills and awareness of people and team behaviours.

Be cautious when you drop the Tech Lead role to play the full-time developer. Broader issues may remain unnoticed and escalate unobserved until they are too big to solve quickly.

Making Yourself Redundant

The newer Tech Lead (mistakenly) sees their role as a person with the deepest technical skills. They think they must have the final say on technical decisions, and must solve *all* of the most difficult technical problems.

These interviews highlight how the Tech Lead is rarely the person with the deepest technical skills. An effective Tech Lead must be technical enough to facilitate meetings with developers, or find ways to resolve disagreements on technical matters. However many Tech Leads wrote about trying to constantly find ways to delegate responsibilities to their team.

When a Tech Lead decides on all the tough problems or keeps all the interesting work, the following scenarios could arise:

- A person starts to feel they are doing all the "boring work" and decides there are more interesting opportunities elsewhere
- A person feels as though they are not valued for making important decisions, and seeks a place they are more valued
- Key decisions stall because they wait for the Tech Lead, who is busy with other responsibilities
- As a Tech Lead, you feel stressed because everyone is constantly asking for you to make a decision

To resolve a decision-making bottleneck, the Tech Lead finds ways to delegate this to the team. Effective delegation means assigning the right person to the task. This requires trust between the Tech Lead and their developers and understanding what skills and knowledge each person has. An effective Tech Lead constantly works towards this.

If you are the Tech Lead and the most technically competent person, you should start growing others so you can delegate decisions in the future. In anything other than the smallest of teams, you cannot design and implement functionality and cover the other Tech Lead responsibilities effectively.

Using Your Own Strengths

All these interviews highlight how people approach the Tech Lead role in many different ways. Each person discovered their own strengths and found a way to put them to use. They also found that some tasks did not play to their strengths but still needed doing. Use books like StrengthsFinder 2.0 to learn more about yourself.

Some Tech Leads have strengths in communication. They develop strong relationships with business people because they easily translate technical matter in ways that non-technical people find simple to understand. Their communication skills help them harmonise the team working towards the same goal and clearly articulate when things go wrong.

Other Tech Leads have strengths in seeing the future. They are better at projecting the future impact of decisions and easily manage Technical Debt. They know when to invest time in burning technical issues, or when to shift into "getting stuff done" mode.

Perhaps a Tech Lead is strong in relationships, both understanding the conflicts emerging in the team, closely getting to know each person, their hopes and goals and finding ways to align individual and team objectives. They understand the need to develop their people, and create a safe nurturing environment.

Spend time understanding yourself. Then spend time finding ways to apply those strengths to the role of Tech Lead to make it your own.

Managing Yourself – Stephen Hardisty

What should a Tech Lead focus on and why?

As you move up the Tech Leadership ladder, you are given more responsibility and a different kind of control. As a developer, you are responsible for coming up with neat solutions to well-defined problems; as Tech Lead, you are responsible for coming up with large solutions to often ill-defined problems. This means you are setting out a vision and relying on others to write the code that implements this vision, which can be frustrating to begin with.

It is important to resist the temptation to step in and take over. Instead, you have to exercise the new control you have inherited: to make the developers around you better. The willingness and ability to make the people around you better at their jobs makes the difference between a mid-level and a senior developer. The great thing about making people better at their job is that it helps you understand who on the team is motivated by a challenge and self-improvement and who is content with being adequate.

The next hurdle is defining "better". In raw terms, it often means delivering at a predictable rate, rarely screwing up, delivering something that people love to use and helping others achieve all of these. However, these are not particularly useful instructions. You need to work out what behaviours need to be encouraged to achieve these things, such as a reasoned approach to testing, empathy for users, and pushing code frequently to reduce risk and gain rapid feedback. As well as being a great way to write code, pair programming is an opportunity to demonstrate these behaviours. You should take the time to either lead by example or couple developers together so that they teach each other the skills you feel they need to improve.

One of the factors that makes you a Tech Lead is that you are clever, but this does not mean you are always right! When discussing solutions with the team, make sure all parties listen to each other politely and all solutions are explored.

The bigger solutions addressing a secondary problem that may come up in future should be treated with caution. If the solution results in you doing more work now in order to factor in something that may not happen, there is a strong chance that you are over-engineering. The only sort of future-proofing that really works is meaningful tests and as little code as possible.

What has been your biggest challenge as a Tech Lead?

The most difficult situation I experienced happened a few years ago. I planned, promoted and started a project that I thought would require four developers and run for about five months.

For a few weeks we felt everything was going smoothly. My manager must have thought otherwise and, to my surprise, added a second Tech Lead and five more developers to the project. I wouldn't want to suggest that the other Tech Lead was wrong or that he was anything but a pleasant person, but we often disagreed with each other's technical decisions. No matter how much discussion happened behind closed doors; how many respected opinions were garnered; how much evidence was produced, we stuck to our diametrically opposing views. The disagreements often resulted in confusion between developers and public disputes between the other Tech Lead and me. This killed morale.

Predictably, the project was technically complex, late, expensive, and now requires a special sort of developer for maintenance: a developer that shares both my skill set and that of the other Tech Lead.

Although this experience was unpleasant, it gave me the opportunity to reflect on how I should behave publicly under difficult circumstances. It taught me that personnel and technical decisions that are hard to justify should be revisited and, of course, that there should not be more than one Tech Lead on a confined project.

There is a positive side to this story. The frustration of a project that initially excited me but eventually turned sour prompted me to make a decision I had been pondering for months: to find another job. I have never regretted this decision and I suspect the project I left behind continued on a much calmer and more focused path without me.

Any time-management tips?

The four main time sinks for me are:

- Reading email
- Attending meetings
- Managing and directing developers
- Writing code

As we all know, email can be a distraction - no matter how important the content. I have two techniques for prioritising email. For low-priority emails, such as certain types of global emails, I have them marked automatically as "read" and only glance at them if I have time. For other emails, I have a different colour for client emails that come to me directly, emails that come to my team, and other emails. This helps me decide quickly how long I should read an email for - from thoroughly understanding to just a simple glance. For the emails that deserve a response, I always respond as quickly as I can to avoid a backlog. This not only keeps me from being overwhelmed but also gives the sender the immediate response they hopefully appreciate.

As for meetings, I am lucky enough to work for a company where all-hands are also broadcast via the internet. Unless my attendance is mandatory, I treat these like a radio and listen to them whilst doing other work. At Etsy we also have what we call the "Fixler rule" (named after one of our directors, Eric Fixler). This rule dictates that you may politely exit when a meeting has ceased to yield value for you. I hold developer weekly one-to-ones and they last for as long as they need to. They are important and non-negotiable. If you want your developers to use up less of your time, the one-to-one is the perfect forum for listening to their concerns and helping them plan self-improvement.

I will leave the code part brief: it is part-time and I

use it as both a way to relax and to keep in touch with how the product and developers are developing. I only ever pick very small, trivial tasks and never anything critical as I cannot guarantee my time.

Outside the nine-to-five (or eight-to-eight!), it is important to have a healthy work/life balance. You should emotionally detach from your work in your spare time as much as possible. If work becomes your main emotional investment, you risk judging your overall success as a human being by your ability to deliver software. Ironically, stress and long hours make you less effective at your job and, whether you like it or not, you set an example to your colleagues.

How do you strike the right balance between writing code and dealing with other issues?

Over time I have become more comfortable with not coding. I still write code but it's generally limited to non-critical changes so I can keep in touch with how things are going overall by working on tasks that do not make me a dependency. There are occasions when something unplanned arises and while the other developers are heads down in their own work, I can shuffle things around and have a crack at the problem. I have learned that these are not occasions to demonstrate that "I still have the magic", but to work out what things could be improved and to run my own mini post-mortem.

Initially I felt my non-coding responsibilities were in addition to writing code. Steadily, the realisation has sunk in that my efforts should instead be focused on trying to make the people I rely on as effective, challenged and motivated as possible.

Stephen's key question: What are some common pitfalls and how can you avoid them?

Single Points of Failure are sometimes difficult to avoid. Some developers love to "own" their work. Although taking responsibility is clearly a good thing, the perception of ownership often leads to one person holding exclusive knowledge of something. The risk of having one developer be the only person to understand something complex is obvious, but you have to be incredibly diligent to avoid it. There are a few ways to prevent *Single Points of Failure* but my preference is to make sure the developer with exclusive knowledge for a given area of code is quickly moved on to something else so another person can take on the challenge. A less jarring solution is pair programming, as long as both developers take fair turns on the keyboard and both understand what is being done.

Another pitfall can be decisions driven without reason. Gut instinct is a marvellous thing and knee-jerk reactions are sometimes your experience subconsciously popping up to tell you something. However, you should understand and be able to explain that reaction before acting upon it. Then there is the other type of irrational decision, and this is worse: decisions driven by ego. It is important to create an atmosphere where it is ok to be wrong. A blameless culture is an enormous asset to sensible decision-making.

Stephen's background story

Stephen has been a software engineer in some capacity for 15 years. He started working at Logica in Bristol, UK, when he was 18, helping to write real-time billing systems. Since then he has worked for MessageLabs (now part of Symantec); for a UK start-up writing anti-spam software; as a Tech Lead for realestate.com.au in Melbourne, Australia, and is currently an engineering manager at Etsy in New York. He has been building and managing teams for about seven years and has realised that he prefers to work with small teams on highly focused goals.

Scouting – Geoffrey Giesemann

What should a Tech Lead focus on and why? The Tech Lead role can vary widely, depending on the composition of the team and the organisational context the team is in. I like to think of a Tech Lead as the scout for a team. They're the person you can send ahead of the main body of work to survey the landscape, spot obstacles, come back and report on where the team should head next.

To me, the key responsibility of a Tech Lead lies along this scouting metaphor. For any given project you'll need to make a bunch of technical decisions and the information you need to make those decisions is scattered. Some of it may even be outside the company, in the heads of your customers or peers in other companies. As a Tech Lead you need to ferret out this information and make it available to your team.

If you're in a large organisation, the same responsibility works in reverse. If your team is doing work, odds are the work will impact on a number of other development teams in the organisation. As a Tech

Lead you should be making other teams aware of all the significant changes your team is making so that they can take them into account when they're doing their work.

What has been your biggest challenge as a Tech Lead?

The project I am currently on is quite large (about 12 months) and we're engaged with multiple stakeholders from different parts of the business. The classic problem with multiple stakeholders is that they all want different things and it is up to us to juggle them, along with our own priorities, as we do our work.

In this specific case there are two outcomes: one is to replace a legacy system with a newer, sparkly, better-performing one; the other is to make our customers happier by providing them with better tooling and make part of our system more transparent. Although both outcomes are related (working on the same system), they're completely orthogonal and could be run as two separate projects.

As a result, we have to periodically tack between the outcomes to appease the different parties, and the inefficiencies and delays this causes drive me nuts.

I cannot say I've handled it well, but at the end of the day your project stakeholders are human beings too, and it is important you don't let discontent with their world view breed into hate. A particular bugbear I notice, is when IT people wave their hands dismissively when they refer to the non-IT part of the company as 'the business'. We all work for the same company; we all (in theory) want the same thing, so it is important to keep that in perspective and not let an us-and-them mentality develop.

Any time-management tips?

Two simple things to focus on are delegation and eliminating useless meetings.

Delegation is simple: do *you* need to do this work or can you hand it over to someone else? (or ignore it completely if it is not important). Sometimes this means handing over work to someone who may not do it as well or may take longer than you would have. These are costs you need to bear and I recommend trying to make it an opportunity for the delegate to learn or upskill in the process.

In terms of meetings (I am echoing Rands here a bit), a meeting is usually called because a bunch of people need to make a decision or to disseminate information. If the purpose of the meeting isn't made clear, or the right mix of people aren't at the meeting, I tend to avoid the meeting or find an excuse to opt out.

How do you strike the right balance between writing code and dealing with other issues?

I still really like writing code - sometimes I take myself off for half a day so I can while away at the keyboard in private. It is going to take a fair bit of effort to drag me further up the management chain.

If I miss out on writing code for an extended period of time, I get grumpy and start taking it out on the team, which is not good. I try to box out time at least once a week so I can do coding on stuff I want to work on. This keeps me happy, and a happy Tech Lead makes for a happier team :)

Geoffrey's key question: Why did you decide to become a Tech Lead?

A myriad of reasons. I think I reached a point where I understood that not all problems can be solved by writing code (and quite a few problems are caused by it) and that it is incredibly important for large groups of developers working in the same domain to work and think in the same direction. If they don't, chaos ensues quickly.

I am also reasonably good at programming things and I figured I could use a challenge.

Geoffrey's other question: When is a developer ready to become a Tech Lead?

In short, when they realise there's no such thing as a bad program.

I was involved with a project at work that required migrating every bit of software ever written at my company to another data centre. This involved reading a lot of code, and modifying it to make previously hard-coded values configurable. During this, I migrated a copy of our main web application that was forked at an earlier stage and used to deliver our content via an alternate channel. Although the code was customised by some inexperienced developers, the fact that it had not undergone any product development or refactoring for 18 months meant that it was actually quite simple and a pleasure to work with. I got it running in about four hours.

This really opened my eyes in that I suddenly understood why software at that company was the way it was and how it got there. It was both euphoric and somewhat depressing at the same time.

Geoffrey's background story

Geoffrey has played the Tech Lead role for just over two years, leading three different teams. He has worked as a programmer for slightly over seven years, and is now employed by Real Estate Australia in Melbourne. When not found inside programming, Geoffrey enjoys the great outdoors.

Lead from Behind – Joel Tosi

What should a Tech Lead focus on and why?

Ultimately as a Tech Lead, you determine the leader you will be. It is easy to identify what I worry about as a Tech Lead: I don't want to become a dependency or a title. This concern has actually made me consider turning down leadership roles before. When I was first asked to lead the solution architects at Red Hat, I nearly turned it down. I felt that the team was working fine together and there wasn't any need for delineation amongst us. I struggled to see what void a Tech Lead would fill and, more importantly, how it would make the team better.

In hindsight, I realise that was more of a reflection of me than the title or the position. The title of Tech Lead is what you make it (unless your manager uses it as a micro-management tool, which I have seen).

So the most important thing a Tech Lead should focus on is not leading. The word "lead" implies that other people are subservient and following. I prefer to focus on facilitating environments, where we can all learn from each other and everyone can do their best work.

Whether I am helping my team members to review code or architectures or simply listening to them vent, I never want to come across as authoritative, but seek to understand their position. For example, if someone is choosing to use a certain algorithm that I might not agree with, I do my best to understand their thought process in reaching that decision, as opposed to saying, "Well you know, that is $O(n^2)$ and I think you can do it in $O(n)$." That is nonsense.

What has been your biggest challenge as a Tech Lead?

When I was first leading a team, we faced a ridiculous project deadline. I know that happens everywhere, but imagine if you would, a project where, at inception you estimate it will be a year of work, but the reality is you are to go live in four months. The solution you are offered is to bring in more developers. So I went from being a member of a small, four-person team to leading a 10-person team (six consultants). Of course, as the lead, I had to make sure the new consultants were immediately productive, the existing team understood what to do, finish my own code, and design the next phases.

In brief: we failed miserably. We went to production on time, after working an average of 80 hours a week (one week, we maxed out at 102 hours) and after being in production for about eight hours, the project was rolled back. Then the post-mortems started, more developers were thrown at the problem, and it continued to spiral. Eventually, after about two more months of scrambling, we got management to understand that we needed to slow down and focus on the quality of our code, integration, and environments.

How did I handle the situation? Well, based on the project outcome, pretty poorly. We ran code reviews; I tried to get the team to understand testing and dependencies, etc. I tried to impose quality and learning new frameworks (REST back then, Maven build, as well as first revision of JQuery, not to mention messaging to people who had never worked with a Notifier model before) and it blew up.

On the upside: no one quit. We had a strong team that bonded through it all. We have all moved on, and I still speak with the majority of that team. So maybe I didn't do as badly as I think I did.

Any time-management tips?

It depends on the organisation and role I am in. When I first became a lead, I thought that being busy in meetings meant I was protecting my team, as well as doing the important, busy work.

Later, I started blocking out time on my calendar for team time. And even later, I started blocking out some time for 'me' time.

These days, I set myself reminders for team interactions. I just ramped up a new member of a team - a process that lasts upwards of eight weeks. Even though that has ended, I have set a reminder to myself to check in on him every 2 weeks, just to see how he is doing. It can be about code, architecture, certainly, but first and foremost it is about him and how he is doing. If you don't work with your peers as people, then you have already lost.

So I have personal reminders to interact not only within my team, but also outside of my team. I may not hit them all the time, and it's not as though I am calling people every other week at a certain time - ad hoc is more natural. I still block out time for myself as well; you have to stay sane.

How do you strike the right balance between writing code and dealing with other issues?

Early on, I thought the only issues were code issues. Over the years, I have realised that the majority of our issues are communication issues. So I try to be as effective a listener as possible first, and secondly as effective a communicator as possible.

Honesty, transparency, and humility will always serve you well.

Joel's key question: Why do you want to be a leader?

I want to see others become greater than me and I want to see the team become even better still.

Joel's second key question: What reading would you recommend to other Tech Leads?

Anything by Weinberg is amazing, but if I had to choose one, it would be General Principles of System Design (although Becoming a Technical Leader may also be fitting in this context).

System Design and Thinking has shaped, and continues to shape, not only how I see my interactions with systems, but also my peers and my team. It helps me elevate my team and assist them with questioning and learning what's beyond their initial conception. General Principals of System Design is a book that you can read and understand, then some time later - for me it was about a month - you just get hit. It is like seeing the matrix. I hope others have a similar experience.

Joel's background story

Joel current works as the Tech Lead for Solutions Architects for JBoss North America. He has previously spent time as an agile consultant and XP coach for VersionOne and as a Tech Lead, manager and architect at the Chicago Mercantile Exchange.

Joel's approach as a Tech Lead has evolved from "leading by example" to "leading from behind". His current approach involves more observing and aiding threatening, challenging or questioning and feels his approach makes him more aware as a Tech Lead.

Understand Yourself – Daniel Worthington-Bodart

What should a Tech Lead focus on?

I think it is important to play to your strengths in whatever you do. Be ruthless and unrelenting in the pursuit of that goal, but choose your fights. For myself, I pursue technical excellence above all else, but this is not to say you should too. Make sure you leave room for your teammates to excel in their strengths too.

Another task for the Tech Lead is to unblock your team. Sometimes you will be the hero, but never forget you may also need to be the janitor.

What has been your biggest challenge as a Tech Lead?

The biggest challenges are often the slowest or longest to achieve: I have been working for three years to decouple a number of business critical systems. It has been a long hard slog. As usual, the challenges are both social and technical. The greatest challenge is not losing sight of the goal and constantly putting one foot in front of the other.

I find that technical challenges come hard and fast, but the delivery and organisational challenges that are inevitably entwined make the difference between a long-term solution and a short-term fad. Do not give up!

Any time-management tips?

The best thing I have found is to have a kid; now I hardly need to sleep!

On a more serious note, if you are as disorganised as me, then do not forget to ask for help. Asking for help not only helps you, but also allows other people to step up and share the responsibility.

How do you strike the right balance between writing code and dealing with other issues?

I think we often try and force code out by sitting in front of the keyboard and writing code. Often the breaks we take away from the keyboard allow our subconscious to solve the problem for us. Pair programming also helps enormously as, when you are away, your pair can continue with the direct approach to the problem, while you will come back with fresh eyes and probably a new solution.

I do not think I have found balance, as I am constantly thinking about code or coding. For me, the problem is actually stopping.

Dan's key question: As a Tech Lead, how much do you think your role is actually about technical leadership compared with people leadership? Or, How do you make technical leadership decisions stick in the long-term?

I think the answer is in the question. We can show people great technical leadership and vision, but it takes time for people to gain a deep understanding of problems. We often have to allow people to fail (in a safe manner) so they can feel the tension of forces one has to balance in crafting a solution.

Dan's background story

Dan has been in IT for nearly 18 years, working in all dimensions, from support, networks and infrastructure, quality assurance, technical sales, consultancy and software development that spans over 50 different clients in different industries.

He has played the Tech Lead role most recently in the last seven years for about ten different teams. He loves finding the simple in the complex. When Dan is not writing code, he enjoys music, films and books in addition to a little bit of rock climbing.

Finding Balance – Laura Paterson

What should a Tech Lead focus on and why?

I think this is a really interesting question, and I don't think there is a simple or single answer to it. Of the teams I have led, no two have been similar; each has asked different things of me as a Tech Lead. To me the most important quality required of a Tech Lead is the ability to stand back and see the big picture and then the ability to adapt to fix the most pressing challenge, whether it's architectural considerations, looking at code quality, managing technical stakeholders, team balance, slimming down process, team happiness or identifying potential issues.

In my first Tech Lead role, we were initially developing a research and development system that had many potential business stakeholders. The technology stack was well known, the team was mature and used to working together, so the key challenges I had were identifying which features were going to be most useful and what architecture would ensure the required flexibility.

A more recent gig was kicking off a green-field media project. The client knew what they wanted and had spent a lot of time with a design agency establishing what features they wanted, and we had well defined cross-functional requirements. On this project my main role was guiding the architectural choices, liaising with technical stakeholders, and helping the onshore and offshore teams establish good working practices.

I believe the role of a Tech Lead is not to dictate, but to help the team deliver. The world shouldn't fall apart if the Tech Lead goes on holiday, and the team should feel empowered to make its own choices. The more junior the team, the more the Tech Lead may need to do to guide technical decisions and development practices. A key skill is communicating effectively - both inwards and outwards.

What has been your biggest challenge as a Tech Lead?

I joined a large project as a developer and was quickly asked to become Tech Lead due to someone leaving. The team was large: six or seven developer pairs, the large codebase was a year old and, due to a heavy initial push for delivery, fairly monolithic. The team was lethargic from working in a sprawling codebase for so long, and the large team size had reduced ownership of code and made it difficult to create consistency in code patterns and quality. In addition, there were concerns about meeting some cross-functional requirements (CFRs). Despite blocking out pairing days and trying to come up to speed with Scala, which was new to me, I found myself with little time to spend on the code, so I had to find alternative ways to look at the issues I could see. Luckily I was working with some great lead developers, who knew the codebase well; being able to trust them gave me confidence to look at some of the team-wide issues. We were able to split the team up into three business areas fairly quickly, which improved code ownership and team enthusiasm.

I ran a series of workshops with the business and the team to identify exactly what was required in terms of CFRs, and how far we were from achieving them in the current solution, essentially exposing the hidden technical debt in the system. We looked at 'softer' CFRs such as testability and maintainability as well as more easily measurable ones such as performance. From this we were able to create a technology backlog, with items marked for impact and effort to change. By identifying impact on business, we were able to get the list prioritised, and secure capacity to fix our most significant technical debt.

Any time-management tips?

I've tried many things! Sticky notes, the Pomodoro Technique, mind maps, blocking out time in my diary to give me time away from the BAU, and identifying pairing days. What currently works for me is checking my calendar and reading my email before I leave the house in the morning. This brings me up to date with anything that may have happened overnight or anything that I need to do in the day. I let this percolate on the journey to work so that by the time I get to work I have a pretty good idea in my head of what I want to achieve in the day. Then I write it down! Sometimes on stickies, sometimes in Evernote. Whenever I do anything, I write it up in Evernote. This lets me move on to the next goal on my list. I have a shocking memory, so everything gets written down. I can add to my list in the day, as things come up, but by having a list, I can see what gets bumped off the bottom and make sure it happens the next day. If something gets bumped too often, I make a call on whether I need to do it or can someone else do it, or can I bin it. Sometimes the important has to take precedence over the urgent; writing it down helps me understand how to create that balance.

How do you strike the right balance between writing code and dealing with other issues?

This is something I've battled with since my first Tech Lead role eight years ago. It is easy on a small team, but gets harder as more developers or political factors come into play. On more complex teams I find it difficult to retain a broader perspective if immersed in a story. I think, at best, this is an area that can only be mitigated. To do this effectively, I ask myself, on this project, what are the benefits I hope to get from pairing, and what is the best way to realise them. Some usual benefits are: understanding the codebase, developing skills in junior developers, aligning development with architectural vision, to feel pain first hand. Pairing may be the best way to reap these benefits, but if this is not possible, what other tools can be utilised? Reviewing code changes to keep current with the code base. Weekly tech reviews, and daily tech huddles give an opportunity for pairs to share their achievements and concerns with the team. In fact, this goes back to my previous answer about what is important to a Tech Lead. The key thing for me is to maintain a clear overall vision of the project and not to lose sight of that when responding to the daily ebb and flow of a project.

Laura's key question: What would you have done differently the first time you stepped into the Tech Lead role?

I wish I'd asked for more help. In the first couple of projects I led, I tried to do everything myself: writing code, organising a test strategy as we had no separate QAs, and validating requirements as it was the good old waterfall days. Luckily the team was small and well formed, so we were able to deliver. But I was exhausted, and it was not an enjoyable experience for me or the team.

It was a desire to learn the art of delegation in the second of these gigs that started me on my journey in agile.

Laura's background story

Laura has a rich and varied history with a background in English Literature and Economics before transitioning into IT. She has played the Tech Lead role for about eight teams since then in a variety of industries including media, publishing, telecommunications, defence, banking, and charities.

She has a strong interest in using agile practices to unlock the potential in the teams she works with.

Conclusions

When I started this book project, I wasn't sure what sort of responses people would give, nor was I sure if there would be any interest in this topic. As I shared the idea with developers and potential interview candidates, the questions I posed puzzled them because they could not name many books that tackled these important issues.

Many people could reel off books and resources that described how to write better code or how to design and build robust applications. Other people knew of books and resources that taught general leadership, communication, and management theory, but developers and Tech Leads expressed frustration about their generality, lack of context, and not necessarily being entirely relevant to the Tech Lead role.

After reading through the responses in one sitting, I was fascinated by how frequently certain themes emerged and how people would return to the same topics time and time again. In this section, I summarise those recurrent themes and how they shed light on different aspects to the Tech Lead role.

Lessons Learned by First-Time Tech Leads

The transition from a role where you exclusively write code to one where writing code is only a small part is what often takes people by surprise. Here are lessons the First-Time Tech Leads touched upon:

- **Having a broader outlook** - Moving beyond the thoughts of a single feature, or code and seeing the whole breadth of the team and business.
- **Sensing greater responsibility** - The authority that comes with the title requires greater accountability; you are accountable not only for your decisions, but the decisions and actions of each person on the team.
- **Guiding the technical vision** - The combination of more responsibility and a broader outlook gives rise to concerns when individuals move in different directions. You spend more time providing direction from a technical point of view.
- **Coping with less time writing code** - You have to redefine how you bring value to the team. You have to look at how you enable others to contribute quality code that requires little

rework and delivers to business needs rather than the amount of code or features you deliver.
- **Juggling more context switches** - The Tech Lead role challenges your time and task-management capabilities as more people will interrupt you for clarification, guidance, and advice. Burning issues draw you away from code-writing, so you need to beware of contributing to the critical path or holding unique knowledge from the team.
- **Allowing people to fail** - You cannot be everywhere at once and, as much as you want to tell people the traps to avoid, you have to accept that sometimes people learn best by failing. Instead you ensure failure has a small impact by improving the speed of feedback loops.
- **Realising people aspects are hard** - As a developer, you deal with computers for most of the time. You can act grumpily and the computer doesn't react. You realise that everyone is unique and so reacts differently to your interactions. Suddenly you are responsible for resolving conflicts when, before, you could silently slip away.

Lessons Learned by Practising Tech Leads

The seasoned Tech Lead has worked with several teams, possibly across different organisations. Their commentary often represents wisdom gained from making mistakes and learning from them, having had a chance to apply those lessons in a new context. The lessons learned from Practising Tech Leads are summarised below.

People

- **Remaining technically grounded** - Other developers respect you more if you still write code with the team. Your understanding of the issues also improves if you have contact with the code.
- **Finding and developing good people** - As a Tech Lead you are responsible for hiring a great team. You cannot rely on hiring people in an ever-changing market and so you need to develop the people in your team and create an environment that encourages learning.
- **Listening to the team** - As a developer, you probably spend most of your time giving opinions. Your Tech Lead role requires you to now

listen to all the opinions and find the best solution within this cacophony.
- **Appreciating individual strengths** - You will appreciate and sometimes be frustrated by the way people behave differently. You start to recognise different strengths and find ways and situations where people's these are best applied.

The "Tech" of a Tech Lead

- **Guiding the technical solution** - A Tech Lead is responsible for everyone sharing the same technical vision. You use architecture diagrams and whiteboard sessions to help build a shared understanding within the team to help align people.
- **Harmonising team direction** - Nothing is more destructive in a development team than conflict that resolves itself through the source control system, with different opinions expressed through snide commit messages, or by overwriting someone else's style. A Tech Lead detects conflicts and differences in direction and facilitates the team to get back on track.
- **Managing technical risks** - Software has so many potential traps and someone must ensure they don't get forgotten. Your role as a Tech

Lead is to find ways to create visibility and shared understanding of technical risks and to find ways as a group to address them.
- **Taking a longer-term view** - Developers are more likely to focus on a very narrow view of their feature or contribution. Tech Leads worry more about how the choices of today will turn into the problem areas of tomorrow.

Bridging the Business with Tech

- **Building trust** - As a developer, you spend most of your time in the details, interacting with people from other parts of the business just enough to work out what you need to build the right feature. As you move into the Tech Lead role, you spend more time building relationships with key business stakeholders; becoming the "go-to" person from the technical team.
- **Finding time for technology** - Bowing to the pressures from the business to add more features is easy. Ensuring that it is done in a sustainable way is one key challenge that the Tech Lead balances. Having a strong trust with the business makes this possible and translating the benefits of investing in technology helps build better understanding.

- **Making technology solutions easy to understand** - Software is complex in many ways, filled with terminology, constantly changing brands and ideas. As an experienced Tech Lead, you know how to simplify the technical solution and can find analogies or stories to help non-technical people understand the technical landscape enough to help them make better decisions.
- **Influencing planning** - When you have built strong trust and skill in simplifying technical ideas, you will inevitably be drawn into more future-focused sessions that might involve budgeting or project planning, because people see yours as an important component. You balance this carefully because more time away from the team reduces the freshness of your own information.
- **Championing business needs** - Sometimes technology teams drift away from understanding end users and the business models that serve them. Tech Leads bring that bigger picture back to the team, clarify how technical solutions impact end users, and what the business goals are. The team makes much better software design choices with this knowledge.

You

- **Adapting to new circumstances** - From the responses in this book, you can see how many diverse situations Tech Lead may find themselves in and the richness of skills needed to deal with them. You must find ways to build skills you may never have had a chance to develop before.
- **Making yourself redundant** - Although you may find it easy to play the "Hero Tech Lead" who does everything on their own, it is not sustainable over the long term, nor does it scale to a bigger team. You focus on developing people and finding ways to delegate tasks so that you can spend more time "just being a developer".
- **Using your own strengths** - Everyone has their own approach to being a Tech Lead, and when thrust into this role, you spend more time introspecting about what you can offer and apply it generously.

Final Words

I hope that you have enjoyed reading the stories from the people in my book as much as I enjoyed gathering and reflecting on them. Some people's stories may have resonated more strongly than others, and if you find yourself in different circumstances, I would encourage you to read the stories afresh as you may find that someone else's stories resonate more than they did previously.

I hope my book has helped to give you a clearer understanding of what a Tech Lead role does. The Tech Lead role is very different from that of a developer. You suddenly have to balance depth of technical understanding with the people side and find time to build relationships with the business. You face new challenges building these new skills. You suddenly find yourself responsible for more people than just yourself and you discover that there is rarely any "right" answer when it comes to people.

Fortunately, you are not the first to embark on taking on this role and, with this collection of stories and lessons in hand, you will be better prepared for it.

Appendix

Useful Books

Allen, David: *Getting Things Done: The Art of Stress-Free Productivity*, Penguin Books, 2002.

Ayres, Ian: *Carrots and Sticks: Unlock the Power of Incentives to Get Things Done*, Bantam, 2010.

Beck, Kent and Martin Fowler: *Planning Extreme Programming*, Addison-Wesley Professional, 2000.

Beck, Kent: *Test Driven Development: By Example*, Addison-Wesley Professional, 2002.

Benson, Jim and Tonianne DeMaria Barry: *Personal Kanban: Mapping Work | Navigating Life*, CreateSpace Independent Publishing Platform, 2011.

Brooks, Jr., Frederick P.: *The Mythical Man-Month: Essays on Software Engineering, Anniversary Edition*, Addison-Wesley Professional, 1995.

Brown, Simon: *Software Architecture for Developers*[22],

---

[22]https://leanpub.com/software-architecture-for-developers

Leanpub, 2012.

Cohn, Mike: *Agile Estimating and Planning*, Prentice Hall, 2005.

Derby, Esther and Johanna Rothman: *Behind Closed Doors: Secrets of Great Management*, Pragmatic Bookshelf, 2005.

Ellnestam, Ola and Daniel Brolund: *The Mikado Method*, Manning Publications, 2013.

Evans, Eric: *Domain-Driven Design: Tackling Complexity in the Heart of Software*, Addison-Wesley Professional, 2003.

Foote, Brian and Joseph Yoder: *A Big Ball of Mud*, Fourth Conference on Patterns Languages of Programs (PLoP '97/EuroPLoP '97), Monticello, Illinois, September 1997.

Gamma, Erich, Richard Helm, Ralph Johnson and John Vlissides: *Design Patterns: Elements of Reusable Object-Oriented Software*, Addison-Wesley Professional, 1994.

Gladwell, Malcolm: *Blink: The Power of Thinking Without Thinking*, Back Bay Books, 2007.

Gray, Dave, Sunni Brown and James Macanufo: *Gamestorming: A Playbook for Innovators, Rulebreakers, and*

Changemakers, O'Reilly Media, 2010.

Lopp, Michael: *Managing Humans: Biting and Humorous Tales of a Software Engineering Manager*, Apress, 2012.

Osherove, Roy: *Notes to a Software Team Leader*, Team Agile Publishing, 2013.

Osherove, Roy: *The Art of Unit Testing: With Examples in .NET*, Manning Publications, 2013.

Patterson, Kerry, Joseph Grenny, Ron McMillan and Al Switzler: *Crucial Conversations: Tools for Talking When Stakes Are High, Second Edition*, McGraw-Hill, 2011.

Pink, Dan: *Drive: The Surprising Truth About What Motivates Us*, Riverhead Books, 2011.

Rath, Tom: *StrengthsFinder 2.0*, Gallup Press, 2007.

Reynolds, Garr: *Presentation Zen: Simple Ideas on Presentation Design and Delivery*, New Riders, 2011.

Rosenberg, Marshall B. and Arun Gandhi: *Nonviolent Communication: A Language of Life*, Puddledancer Press, 2003.

Spence, Gerry: *How to Argue & Win Every Time: At Home, At Work, In Court, Everywhere, Everyday*, St. Martin's Griffin, 1996.

Weinberg, Gerald M.: *Becoming a Technical Leader*,

Dorset House Publishing, 1986.

Weinberg, Gerald M and Daniela Weinberg: *General Principles of System Design*, Dorset House Publishing, 1988.

Wilde, Gerald J.S.: *Target Risk 2: A New Psychology of Safety and Health*, Pde Pubns, 2001.

Useful Websites

Personal Kanban[23]

Inbox Zero[24]

Getting Things Done[25] Rands[26]

---

[23] http://www.personalkanban.com

[24] http://inboxzero.com

[25] http://gettingthingsdone.com

[26] http://randsinrepose.com

Other References

Foote, Brian and Joseph Yoder: *A Big Ball of Mud*, Fourth Conference on Patterns Languages of Programs (PLoP '97/EuroPLoP '97) Monticello, Illinois, September 1997.

Linux Magazine[27]

Communications of the ACM[28]

---

[27] http://www.linux-magazine.com

[28] http://cacm.acm.org

About the Author

When this book was being put together, I was working as a Principal Consultant for ThoughtWorks, where you would find me leading teams and striving to create great environments where developers could thrive, always focused on delivering value to end users. I have a great interest in balancing the people side to software development, as well as the challenge and enjoyment of solving hard technical problems. And yes, I still write code too and love it.

I am passionate about improving teams through the use of Retrospectives[29] and growing individuals. I have coached a number of developers into the role of being a Tech Lead and I hope this book helps you grow your mastery as a Tech Lead or better prepares you for the start of your journey as a Tech Lead.

---

[29] http://leanpub.com/the-retrospective-handbook

Printed in Great Britain
by Amazon.co.uk, Ltd.,
Marston Gate.